KU-225-819

FORM AND PURPOSE IN BOSWELL'S
BIOGRAPHICAL WORKS

FORM AND PURPOSE
IN BOSWELL'S
BIOGRAPHICAL WORKS

By William R. Siebenschuh

UNIVERSITY OF CALIFORNIA PRESS
BERKELEY · LOS ANGELES · LONDON
1972

University of California Press
Berkeley and Los Angeles
California
❖
University of California Press, Ltd.
London, England

ISBN: 0-520-02246-7

LIBRARY OF CONGRESS CATALOG CARD NO. 74-171621

© 1972 BY THE REGENTS OF THE UNIVERSITY OF CALIFORNIA
PRINTED IN THE UNITED STATES OF AMERICA

ACKNOWLEDGMENTS

THIS ESSAY in its present form or perhaps any other would not have been possible without the guidance, assistance, and encouragement of Professor Ralph W. Rader. Any value that it may have will be due in large part to the interest he took in it and the critical attention he gave to every aspect of its conception, composition, and revision—both as a dissertation and in its present form. Professors Brendan O'Hehir and Thomas Barnes, who read it as a dissertation, were extremely helpful, as was Professor Bertrand Bronson, who was good enough to read and criticize the chapter on the *Tour to the Hebrides*. He made a number of valuable suggestions which I have attempted to incorporate. Others whose assistance was important were John Buck, Maurice Hunt, Martin Reutinger, and last but certainly not least my wife Sandra, who was my editor, typist, proofreader, and captive audience. I could not have completed it without her assistance and encouragement.

W. R. S.

CONTENTS

INTRODUCTION

Boswell's methods for dramatizing his primary factual materials have been studied carefully in the *Life of Johnson*, but they have not been dealt with systematically or comparatively in what are generally considered to be his three major biographical works: the portrait of Paoli in the *Account of Corsica*, the *Tour to the Hebrides*, and the *Life of Johnson*. The purpose of this examination will be to make a beginning toward such a comparative study. The formal and, more important, the stylistic differences among the biographical portraits in these works provide new evidence for the growing estimate of Boswell's artistic abilities in general, and about the nature and extent of his achievement in the *Life of Johnson* in particular.

It has always been felt that there was very little difference in the way Boswell dramatized his primary factual material in each of his major biographical works. In terms of structure and style the *Account of Corsica* and the *Tour to the Hebrides* have been for the most part unexamined. To the extent that a critical tradition about the literary relationship among them can be said to exist at all it can be summarized rather briefly. Boswell is presumed to have discovered his talent for biography at the time he wrote the *Account of Corsica*. In the *Tour to the Hebrides* he is thought to have fully realized and proven his special powers as a biographer of Johnson and to have discovered the full potential of Johnson as a biographical subject. The *Life* is considered to be a full-length treatment of Johnson in the same style that Boswell discovered in the *Account* and perfected in the *Tour*. There is little in the way of comparative criticism of these works that goes beyond the idea that Boswell's development as a biographer was a simple, linear progression; that he was good in the *Account of Corsica*, better in the *Tour to the*

Hebrides, and best in the *Life of Johnson.* This states the obvious but explains very little.

George Mallory's early study of Boswell's career as a biographer[1] established this view of it. His discussion of the *Account* and the *Tour* is very brief but his conclusions have been accepted almost without question until recently. He treats the *Account* and the *Tour* only as he believes they demonstrate progressive development of the same artistic methods Boswell was later to use more successfully in the *Life.* "The chief interest of the 'Tour to Corsica,' " he writes, "is that it is the earliest example of Boswell's biographical method. The memoirs we have here of Paoli aim at giving a picture of a man in much the same way as does the 'Life of Johnson.' "[2] Boswell's "method" is discussed in the singular—the possibility of others is not raised. And Mallory does not elaborate on what "much the same way as does the 'Life of Johnson' " means in stylistic terms. Of the *Tour to the Hebrides* he observes only that, " 'The Journal of a Tour to the Hebrides' must be criticized along with the 'Life of Johnson' and not apart from it. It is, in a sense, but a portion of the larger work."[3]

The only other major work to treat all three works together is Mark Longaker's *English Biography in the Eighteenth Century.*[4] But Longaker borrows directly from Mallory and adds nothing new.[5] Early biographies of Boswell (Tinker and Fitz-

---

[1] George Mallory, *Boswell the Biographer* (London, 1912).

[2] Mallory, p. 59.

[3] Mallory, p. 217.

[4] Mark Longaker, *English Biography in the Eighteenth Century* (Philadelphia, 1931).

[5] Following Mallory's lead and sometimes quoting him directly, Longaker writes: "After his success with the *Memoirs of Pascal Paoli,* published in his *Account of Corsica* in 1768, in which his method of reproducing conversation was interestingly employed, Boswell was cognizant of his talent in this direction, and he made of his method in the years following his account of Paoli a perfected part of his biographical equipment. In 1785, when the *Journal of a Tour to the Hebrides* appeared, he em-

gerald)[6] and the other standard studies of biography (Dunn, Johnston, Lee, Nicolson, and Garraty)[7] also follow Mallory's lead, and most give the two earlier works only a passing mention at best. In the standard critical edition of the *Tour to the Hebrides*[8] the only comment that deals formally with the structure or style of the work is that it is an "essay in Johnsonian biography."[9] And Donald Stauffer in his impressive study, *The Art of Biography in Eighteenth Century England*,[10] discusses the *Life of Johnson* almost exclusively and does not discuss the *Account* or the *Tour* separately.

---

ployed essentially the same perfected method that he was to use so effectively in the *Life of Johnson*" (p. 435). The discussion goes no further in examining Boswell's dramatic and representational techniques than to say that his method of reproducing Paoli's conversation was "interestingly employed." The basic idea of discovery of a talent in the *Account*, development in the *Tour*, and perfection in the *Life* is reasserted with next to no examination of the two earlier works.

[6] The two best biographies prior to Frederick A. Pottle's exhaustive work now in progress are C. B. Tinker, *Young Boswell* (Boston, 1922) and Percy Fitzgerald, *The Life of Boswell*, 2 vols. (London, 1912).

[7] The standard general studies of English biography are Sir Sidney Lee, *The Principles of Biography* (Cambridge, 1911); Waldo Dunn, *English Biography* (New York, 1916); J. D. Johnston, *Biography: The Literature of Personality* (New York, 1927); Sir Harold Nicolson, *The Development of English Biography* (New York, 1928); and John Garraty, *The Nature of Biography* (New York, 1957). Harold Nicolson's treatment of Boswell is the fullest, but he does little more than repeat the common view: "What he calls the 'peculiar plan of this biographical undertaking' [the *Life*] had remained in his mind for over twenty-five years. He experimented with it, not very successfully in his early Corsican journal; he gave it a trial in his *Journal of a Tour to the Hebrides*." (p. 106).

[8] *Boswell's Life of Johnson together with Boswell's Journal of a Tour to the Hebrides and Johnson's Diary of a Journey into North Wales*, ed. G. B. Hill, Revised and Enlarged by L. F. Powell, Vol. V, 6 vols. (Oxford, 1964).

[9] *Tour to the Hebrides*, p. vi.

[10] Donald Stauffer, *The Art of Biography in Eighteenth Century England* (Princeton, 1941).

It has not been lack of interest in the works themselves that has been responsible for the dearth of structural and stylistic comparisons among them. Rather, some widely accepted ideas about the limits of Boswell's abilities as a literary artist and biographer have prevented certain questions being asked. Although recent criticism has given Boswell the credit he deserves as a literary artist, it is still felt that he was able to exercise very little organizational and interpretive power over the primary factual material that he dealt with. Donald Stauffer suggests, "Boswell had a mind neither original enough nor powerful enough to distort actual events to fit a preconception or a spiritual need."[11] And the best of more recent studies suggests strongly that he had neither the ability nor the design of imposing more than an accidental or coincidental artistic unity upon any of his works, or of developing his factual materials with the intention of producing a larger than local literary effect.[12]

Along with this idea has gone the view that great as his abilities were he was an essentially mechanical, not an interpretive, biographer, and was limited artistically by his zeal for factual accuracy. "Boswell distrusted interpretive and imaginative biography," writes Stauffer. "But interpretation and imagination are qualities of the artist, and Boswell's *Life* gains as a record of fact sometimes at the expense of art. Instead of creating John-

---

[11] Stauffer, p. 413.

[12] The clearest and most concise statement of this view is Professor Bertrand Bronson's in "Samuel Johnson and James Boswell," *Facets of the Enlightenment* (Berkeley, 1968), p. 226. "His power of invention," writes Mr. Bronson, "and his shaping hand operate on events themselves and not primarily on the literary product. . . . Boswell seldom labored at the realization of a larger unity than life was ready to offer. . . . His best achievements have a unity for which he is only indirectly responsible. The *London Journal,* the *Corsica* episode, the account of his visits to Voltaire and Rousseau, the *Tour to the Hebrides,* and the *Life of Johnson* have the kind of coherency and completeness that sufficed him: a unity comprised of chronological sequences or scenes, beginning and ending at fixed moments of historical time and connected by a personal identity."

son, it affords material from which Johnson may be created by an imaginative act."[13] "What he needs," writes Joseph Wood Krutch, "is not imagination or insight, or even primarily the judgment to select. It is documentation and more documentation."[14] Professor Pottle was among the first to underscore Boswell's dramatic abilities—as a journalist and a biographer—and, following Professor Pottle's lead, subsequent critics have conceded much greater imaginative powers to him.[15] But there has been a surprising unwillingness until very recently to concede to him more than an absolute minimum of greater than local artistic control of his materials—even in the construction of what is admittedly one of the world's great biographies.[16]

---

[13] Stauffer, pp. 445–446.

[14] Joseph Wood Krutch, *Samuel Johnson* (New York, 1944), p. 386.

[15] In the last few decades there has been strong reaction to what might be termed the Macaulayan version of Boswell's abilities and limitations. Critics like Professors Pottle ("James Boswell, Journalist," *Age of Johnson, Essays Presented to C. B. Tinker*, New Haven, 1949; and "The Life of Boswell," *Yale Review*, 35, 1946); Wimsatt ("James Boswell: The Man and the Journal," *Yale Review*, 49, 1959, 80–92); and Bronson ("Boswell's Boswell," *Johnson Agonistes and Other Essays*, Berkeley, 1965) have shown in some detail the skill with which he was able to dramatize materials for both his journals and his published works. But none of them has suggested the kind of organizational or synthetic abilities that I shall attempt to show he was capable of.

[16] The discovery of the *Malahide Papers* did nothing really to change the general estimate of the nature and extent of Boswell's literary achievement in the *Life*. R. W. Chapman, in a review of the first six volumes of the *Malahide Papers* (including the *Making of the Life of Johnson*) wrote in *TLS*, 6 Feb., 1930: " '. . . when all is said—when the work of revision has been traced through its stages—the conclusion, that issues is the altogether welcome conclusion that there is no surprising revelation. When Boswell's workshop has been ransacked, the results previously reached by scholarship are confirmed. We now know for certain . . . that the finished *Life* is substantially the same thing as the contemporary records. The revision, careful and artful though it was, appears as an operation of polishing, not as a structural synthesis.' " Marshall Waingrow, ed. *The Correspondence and Other Papers Relating to the Making of the Life of Johnson*, Vol. 2, *Yale Edition of the Private Papers of James Boswell* (Research Edition), ed. Frederick A. Pottle, et al. (New York, 1969), p. xxii.

These widely accepted general beliefs about the limits of Boswell's art have, I think, discouraged previous comparative examination of all of his biographical works. If it is felt that none of them is more than accidentally or coincidentally unified, there is presumably little to be gained by close structural comparison. If, as has been asserted, "Boswell's art lies in the organization of the smaller bits of the mosaic; not in the assembling or relating them to one another,"[17] if it is felt that this is the extent of his active role in producing preconceived literary effects in his works, then there would presumably be little to be gained by close stylistic comparison: the artistry in the individual pieces of any of these mosaics should logically be the rough equivalent of that in any of the others. Thus, where structure or style is concerned, to study either of the two earlier works is presumably to study what Boswell did better but not significantly differently in the *Life of Johnson*. But new work done with the *Life of Johnson* has provided evidence that seriously challenges this view of the limits of Boswell's abilities, and it makes a new and closer comparative examination of his earlier biographical works not only legitimate for its own sake but desirable as it might bear directly upon the broader questions of the nature and extent of his talents.

Professor Ralph Rader argues convincingly[18] that Boswell did consciously unify his greatest biographical work, and that the structural principles that controlled his artistic development of his factual materials in it were the cause of its most powerful literary effects. Rejecting the idea that Boswell was a slave to a mechanical, chronological arrangement of data, or that he could make beautiful mosaic pieces but did not consciously organize them, Professor Rader shows that the subject of the *Life* is not

---

[17] Stauffer, pp. 445–446.

[18] Ralph Rader, "Literary Form in Factual Narrative: The Example of Boswell's Johnson," *Essays in Eighteenth Century Biography*, ed. Phillip Daghlian (Bloomington, Indiana, 1968).

Johnson's life but his character; that a coherent concept of Johnson's character in Boswell's own mind and greater than any single incident or episode controlled his artistic development of his factual materials in the work.

Professor Marshall Waingrow's study of Boswell's editorial work with materials about Johnson provided by correspondence with others gives strong support to Professor Rader's thesis. Waingrow shows that Boswell's editorial work with the vast amounts of primary material about Johnson (a large percentage of it consisting of nonverifiable verbal anecdote and reminiscence) was genuine interpretive artistry. "It is evident," he writes, "that Boswell, in editing his authorities, was engaged in more than polishing: he was aiming at a unified and coherent portrait. . . . In so far as the finished *Life* may be supposed to reflect a steadiness of conception, we must assume that the editorial hand which worked upon the source materials was engaged in controlling their effects."[19]

The solid beginnings made by Professors Rader and Waingrow, when combined with the important earlier work done on the *Account of Corsica* by Professor Pottle, suggest that close comparative study of *all* of Boswell's biographical works can provide equally important evidence for a general reassessment of the nature and limits of his abilities as an artist and of his special achievement in the *Life of Johnson*. Professor Pottle is the only critic who has paid close attention to Boswell's literary and dramatic techniques in the portrait of Paoli in the *Account of Corsica*.[20] His work indicates clearly that in important ways Boswell

---

[19] Waingrow, pp. xxxiii and xxxvi.

[20] In the first volume of his new biography of Boswell (*James Boswell: The Earlier Years, 1740–1769,* New York, 1966) and in his Introduction to the excerpted *Memoirs of Pascal Paoli* (*The Yale Edition of the Private Papers of James Boswell,* ed. Frederick A. Pottle, et al., 8 vols., New York, 1950–1963), Professor Pottle shows in greater detail than any previous scholar the extent of the influence of propagandistic motives on the portrait of Paoli. He contrasts Boswell's "Plutarchian Mode" in the portrait

did not use the same literary and dramatic techniques to portray Paoli that he was later to use in the portraits of Johnson. This strongly suggests that there may be greater differences among each of the portraits than has commonly been thought.

Works like those of Professors Rader, Waingrow, and Pottle give rise to some questions that have not been asked of Boswell's early biographical works or about Boswell's career and abilities as a biographer. Most important is the question of whether in fact there *are* important differences among each of the major biographical portraits—and if so, what do they show us about Boswell's abilities as an artist?

Professor Pottle could only discuss Boswell's portrait of Paoli in general terms, and no one has pursued his line of reasoning any further. Boswell's propagandistic motives in the *Account* had an even greater and more pervasive influence upon his development of his factual material than the scope of Professor Pottle's treatment allowed him to suggest. The *Account* does not directly anticipate Boswell's later treatments of Johnson but, in fact, is significantly different from them. And it shows that he was entirely capable of distorting actual events to fit a preconception (to use Stauffer's phrase).

Moreover, Boswell does not portray Johnson in the same way in both the *Tour* and the *Life*. In the *Tour* he juxtaposes an essentially static image of Johnson and the unique environments provided by the tour through the Hebrides. The literary pleasure of the *Tour* is generated to a great extent by the sequence of images of Johnson *being* the Johnson of popular report and affectionate caricature: hating Scotland, laughing at Lord Monboddo and his tail, and defending the Church of England in "the land of John Knox's reformations." But in consistently con-

---

of Paoli with what he terms the "Flemish Style" of the portrait of Johnson in the *Life*. And he suggests differences in Boswell's portrayal of himself as narrator and in his choice of material to be included in conversational sequences.

trasting an essentially static and simplified version of Johnson's character and unusual or contradictory situations, Boswell does not go beyond what amounts (in comparison with the *Life*) to a stereotypic representation of him. He is to be enjoyed as the stern moralist "caught" on a pleasure jaunt; the "champion of the English Tories" in the bed of Flora Macdonald; or the "teacher of moral and religious wisdom" talking about keeping a seraglio. Boswell does not attempt to show us (in the way he is at pains to show us in the *Life*) Johnson in all his complexity and all his intellectual and moral strength. Works like those of Professors Rader and Waingrow go a long way towards explaining in specific terms what has always been felt intuitively: that the *Life of Johnson* is a work of conscious and consummate artistry and not fortunate and remarkable coincidence. And this becomes even clearer and can be explained even more specifically when Boswell's treatment of his materials about Johnson in the *Life* is viewed in *contrast* to his treatment of similar kinds of materials in the *Tour to the Hebrides*.

What emerges from a close comparative study of Boswell's major biographical works is the fact that each is a separate and formally distinct literary achievement. It shows that Boswell does effectively exercise significant organizational powers over the factual materials that are the stuff of his greatest works; and that in the *Life of Johnson*, at least, he was a genuinely interpretive biographer. Seen in contrast to the portrait of Johnson in the *Tour*, Boswell's achievement in the *Life* emerges clearly as a literary creation in every sense of the term that may properly be applied to a factual work.

I. THE *ACCOUNT OF CORSICA*

THE FULL EXTENT to which propagandistic motives affected Boswell's methods for dramatizing his primary factual material throughout the *Account of Corsica* has not been adequately acknowledged even by Professor Pottle, and its importance to a general reassessment of Boswell's biographical career and abilities has not been dealt with. All of the artistic decisions he made in the portrait of Paoli are direct functions of the form and purpose of the *Account* as a whole. It does not directly anticipate his later treatments of Johnson, and it shows that he was able to exercise much greater organizational powers over his factual works than he has generally been thought to have possessed.

The idea of the separability of the portrait of Paoli from the rest of the *Account* on literary grounds began with Johnson. "Your History," he told Boswell, "is like other histories, but your Journal is in a very high degree curious and delightful. There is between the history and the journal that difference which there will always be found between notions borrowed from without, and notions generated within. Your history was copied from books; your journal rose out of your own experience and observation. You express images which operated strongly upon yourself, and you have impressed them with great force upon your readers."[1]

To be sure, that part of the *Account* which deals exclusively with Corsican geography, industry, and natural history was copied from books. The literary quality of the *Account* is much inferior to that of the *Journal and Memoirs*[2] for the very reasons

---

[1] *The Life of Johnson*, II, p. 70.

[2] The text which will be used for all references to the *Account of Corsica* will be the edition of 1769, "The Third Edition Corrected." It has all of Boswell's final corrections and is the edition used as the basis for the parts of the text included in the *Yale Edition of the Private Papers of*

Johnson gives. But although the *Account* is constructed mainly from "notions from without" (to use Johnson's phrase), in important ways it is not, as Johnson would have it, "like other histories."[3] Boswell's literary objective is neither strict factual truth (the historian's and the biographer's objective) nor aesthetic pleasure (the goal of the literary artist). It is persuasion. The *Account* and the *Journal and Memoirs* form a single and continuous piece of propaganda and were intended to function together to influence public opinion in Britain. They present a carefully controlled version of the history and culture of the island and make a plea for direct action by Britain on a specific political issue.

The Introduction to the *Account* strikes the political note that will dominate the work. "Liberty," Boswell begins, "is so natural, and so dear to mankind, whether as individuals, or as members of society, that it is indispensibly necessary to our happiness" (33). One of the major bases of Boswell's strong emotional appeal for the Corsicans is the then-new doctrine of the universal rights of all men to personal liberty and national independence. In a prefatory summary he states the terms in which the Corsicans' struggle is to be viewed and quickly addresses himself to the most important problem they faced in diplomatic terms, formal recognition by the European powers:

---

*James Boswell (Introduction, n. 21). The full title is *An Account of Corsica, The Journal of a Tour to that Island and the Memoirs of Pascal Paoli* (London, 1769). All further quotations will be from this edition and will be referred to by page number at the time of quotation. The various parts of the work—The *Account,* and *Journal and Memoirs*—will be referred to by those names when discussed individually. Reference to the work as a whole will be to the *Account of Corsica.* In the quotations used, Boswell's own spelling and punctuation will be reproduced as it was printed even when it departs from modern usage.*

[3] Boswell's history is not like the new and highly respectable histories that were beginning to be produced at roughly the same time—a comparable account by Hume or Robertson. If it has affinities with other histories at all it is with the "party histories" of the early part of the century.

That the spirit of liberty has flourished in modern times, we may appeal to the histories of the Swiss, and of the Dutch; and the boldest proofs of it are to be found in the annals of our own country.

But a most distinguished example of it actually exists in the island of Corsica. There, a brave and resolute nation, has now for upwards of six and thirty years, maintained a constant struggle against the oppression of the republick of Genoa. These valiant islanders were for a long time looked upon as an inconsiderable band of malcontents, as a disorderly troop of rebels, who would speedily be compelled to resume those chains which they had frowardly shaken off. They have however continued steadily in their purpose. Providence has favoured them; and Europe now turns her eyes upon them, and with astonishment sees them on the eve of emancipating themselves for ever from a foreign yoke, and becoming a free and independent people. (38–39)

In spite of Boswell's phrasing of the matter and his clever use of the past tense ("The valiant islanders *were* for a long time looked upon as a disorderly troop of rebels"), the fact was that they were still considered to be so, at least officially. And as long as they were considered merely rebels or brigands there was no possibility of formal recognition by England. It was perhaps the primary function of Boswell's book to convince the English that Corsica was a genuinely emergent nation state founded upon principles worthy of official recognition. He wanted his readers to do what he claimed all Europe was doing: to view the new state with pleasant surprise on the eve of its hoped-for emancipation from an oppressive foreign yoke (emancipation that would require British intervention).

The appearance of objectivity and factuality is deceptive. It is a necessary one for the sake of the propagandistic purpose of the work, but the rhetorical pattern of the work—both as a whole and in the separate chapters—is to move quickly from the purely (or at least ostensibly) factual to ever more direct and specific political reference. The first chapter, "Of the Situation, Extent, Air, Soil, and Productions, of Corsica," is the only chapter that

really closely approximates Johnson's view of the nature of the
Account as a whole. It is little more than a compilation of data
from external sources, and the efforts to classicize it are almost
painful. But in the second chapter, "A concise View of the Revo-
lutions Which Corsica has undergone from the earliest times,"
Boswell begins to get down to the real business of the work.

He attempts to create the impression of a long tradition
among the Corsicans of struggle against slavery and oppression
in defense of national independence and personal liberty. This
gives the technically false impression that their history (as a
state) is as old and venerable as Rome's herself. "It appears however," he writes, "that the Corsicans could not bear subjection
with patience, for they were continually attempting to get free.
... the Romans never had a firm hold of this country, where the
spirit of liberty, which tyrants call rebellion, was ever breaking
forth" (94–95). In these terms (and they apply throughout the
work) to call the actions of the Corsicans rebellion is to be tyran-
nical. It is a version of the "Emperor's new clothes" technique:
all we (intelligent) readers can see what the Corsicans really are
and stand for—only a tyrant would call them rebels or bar-
barians.

Growing more specific and more topical, Boswell next raises
the omnipresent issue of the natural rights of all men:

Let Corsica have been the property of the Phenicians, the Etrus-
cans, the Carthaginians, the Romans, the Goths, the Saracens: let it
have been a conquest of France; a gift from that kingdom to the pope;
a gift again from the pope to the Pisans, and at length a conquest of
Genoa; still we must have recourse to the plain and fundamental
principle, that the Corsicans are men, and have a right to liberty;
which, if usurped by any power whatever, they have at all times a
just title to vindicate....

For however a people may, from indolence, from timidity, or from
other motives, submit for a season to a certain degre of tyranny; if it
is long continued, and pushed to an exorbitant length, nature will
revolt, and the original rights of man will call for redress. (102–103)

Increasingly direct, Boswell next raises the issue of relatively recent Anglo-Corsican relations. He recalls that earlier, in 1736, the crafty Genoese minister had prevailed upon the crown to prohibit "any of his majesty's subjects from furnishing provisions or assistance to the malcontents of Corsica" (134). (This was roughly the state of things at the time Boswell was writing.) He then tells how an earlier Paoli, General Gaffiori, confronted the Genoese with the resolution of a Roman (148), proving himself worthy of assistance; and how the British at that time were equal to the demands of the situation and rose to the Corsicans' defense in spite of the proclamation forbidding them to do so: "Great Britain had forbidden her subjects to give any assistance to the Corsicans; but by the changeful schemes of political connexions she consented to send some ships against the Genoese. . . . These ships bombarded Bastia, and San Fiorenzo, both of which they delivered into the hands of the Corsicans. The force of the British men of war, and the great service done by us to their cause are never forgotten, by the brave islanders" (149). The significance of the precedent is clear enough, and it leaves open the possibility of either official or unofficial aid. The use of the present tense in the last sentence is important: the deeds of the British "*are* never forgotten, by the brave islanders." The memory is still alive and thus the Corsicans look logically to Britain in the similar situation that now exists.

Pursuing the parallel, Boswell makes Paoli the modern analogue of General Gaffiori. It was important to present Paoli as both a romantic and heroic extension of the virtues of his people and yet a leader both acceptable and admirable by European standards—a man with whom a country like Britain could negotiate formally. He had both to appeal to people's imaginations and still make the appeal valid in practical political terms. In descriptions of the General his superior judgment is stressed along with his heroic carriage and deportment, and the democratic nature of his government is emphasized. Boswell ad-

mitted later that Paoli's rule more resembled a despotism based
on love and trust, but here—to insure maximum acceptability—
he is at great pains to give the impression that in this supposedly
rude nation Paoli was "entirely dependent upon the people,
elected by them, and answerable to them for his conduct" (162).
His efforts towards civilizing and unifying his people are dwelt
upon, and comparisons are made with Lycurgus and the Spartans. He has been able, we are told, at last truly to unite his
people and is leading them in a determined effort to throw off
the yoke of Genoese oppression. He would doubtless have suc-
ceeded already if the French had not intervened. The state of
things at present is a stalemate that can only be broken by British
intervention on the side of the Corsicans. If the British do not
intervene, this brave people must succumb.

Chapter Three, entitled "The present State of Corsica, with
respect to Government, Religion, Arms, Commerce, Learning,
and the Genius and Character of Its Inhabitants," might well
simply have been called "Proof that the Corsicans are Worthy
of Our Aid." As the final chapter of the *Account,* it predictably
contains the most pointed and direct call for political action.
The beginning of the chapter is strictly confined to a discussion
of the structure of the government, the Corsican constitution,
religion, system for taxation, etc. It emphasizes the modernity
of the emergent state. But Boswell shifts quickly into higher
and higher polemical gears. Repeatedly returning to images
of what will be lost if the Corsican state is allowed to fail, he
strongly emphasizes the potential of the island for agricultural
and industrial development and then squarely confronts what
he wants his readers to see as the major obstacle to all this
growth and plenty. "Nothing," he exclaims, "has cast a greater
damp upon the improvements of Corsica, than the King of
Britain's proclamation after the late peace, forbidding his subjects to have any intercourse with that nation" (216). Warming
to his subject, he continues:

I know that if it had not been for this proclamation, the Corsicans would, at the close of the last war, have had several of our stoutest privateers in their service, which would have effectually overawed the Genoese ... And surely it would have been worthy of a people whom the felicity of freedom has rendered generous, to afford their countenance to a race of heroes, who have done so much to secure to themselves the same blessings, especially when our shewing this generosity would greatly coincide with the commercial interests of these kingdoms. (217 misnumbered 214)

Boswell concludes, "When we thus view the Corsicans gloriously striving for the best rights of humanity, and under the guidance of an illustrious commander and able statesman, establishing freedom, and forming a virtuous and happy nation, can we be indifferent as to their success? Can we Britons forbear to admire their bravery, and their wisdom?" (250).

Boswell's history in the *Account* is clearly not primarily an objective factual history or primarily history at all, and the *Journal and Memoirs* is an integral part of this single and continuous piece of propaganda. It confirms, dramatically and with all the force of an ostensibly objective personal record, the image of the Corsican people and of Paoli that has been proposed in the *Account*. Boswell's artistic development of his factual materials in the *Journal and Memoirs* is entirely explainable in terms of its function in relation to the major objectives of the work as a whole: to counter the generally bad impression of the Corsicans by demonstrating their natural simplicity, bravery, and honesty; and to portray Paoli both as an extension of the noblest virtues of his people and at the same time as the distinguished leader of an emergent nation, worthy of formal recognition by Britain. To make his picture of the Corsicans in the *Journal and Memoirs* consonant with the expectations that had been raised in the *Account,* Boswell suppresses material, slants material, and carefully controls his dramatization of conversations and ancedotes. It is not proper to compare his biographical techniques in the *Journal and Memoirs* with the methods he was later to use to portray Johnson, nor to compare his journals here with his usual methods as a journalist.

To counteract the ideas about the rebelliousness and barbarity of the Corsicans, Boswell portrays them throughout in accordance with the most romantic notions of the new doctrines of primitivism. Professor Pottle's discussion of this aspect of the *Journal and Memoirs* is excellent. As he notes, Boswell wanted to portray the Corsicans "as gallant, honest, simple people unjustly deprived of their independence. . . . He softened or suppressed details which would have blurred this image, and emphasized the quasi-idyllic primitivism of an unspoiled race."[4] Beyond this, Boswell consistently blends the best aspects of the new primitivism with classical analogy. The Corsican state is to be seen not merely as a romanticized society of "natives" but (in keeping with the earlier efforts to establish a "classical" history) as a clear analogue of the infancy of the greatest societies of Greece and Rome. Thus, along with direct comparisons between the Corsicans and Rousseau 's idylls, we find anecdotes like that in the great Chancellor's house, which Boswell concludes by observing, "The Chancellor desired a little boy who was playing in the room by us, to run to his mother, and bring the great seal of the kingdom. I thought myself sitting in the house of a Cincinnatus" (310).

Perhaps the most important rhetorical device (outside of the portrait of Paoli himself) is Boswell's portrayal of himself as narrator. Professor Pottle notes that he intentionally gives the impresssion of credulity and naivete to allow himself more freedom to "wonder simply and passionately at the British government."[5] But his use of himself as a naive and somewhat

[4] *Yale Edition of the Private Papers*, IV, p. 147.

[5] *Yale Edition of the Private Papers*, IV, p. 148.

credulous narrator extends well beyond occasions of expressed wonder at British policy. It is one of his most effective devices for showing the Corsicans themselves to advantage.

He comes to the island, we are informed, with all the common European prejudices about the Corsicans. "I recollect with astonishment," he writes, "how little the real state of Corsica was known, even by those who had good access to know it" (292). He sets up a series of situations in which he is guilty of all the common fears and European prejudices about the Corsicans only to have them repeatedly disproved—to his surprise and delight—by their actual behavior whenever he comes into contact with their natural civility, hospitality, and honesty. The naive traveller is continually surprised by civilization he did not expect, hospitality he did not look for, and kindness he does not always deserve. Indeed, his own behavior even causes him some embarrassment: "Before I was accustomed to the Corsican hospitality, I sometimes forgot myself, and imagining I was in a publick house, called for what I wanted, with the tone which one uses in calling to the waiters at a tavern. I did so at Pino, asking for a variety of things at once; when Signora Tomasi perceiving my mistake, looked in my face and smiled, saying with much calmness and good nature, 'One thing after another, Sir' " (301).

The conclusions to be drawn about the "savage" Corsicans are obvious. In fact, by the third or fourth day the situation has become reversed, so that it is Boswell himself who defends the society of the Corsicans to the islanders themselves with all the zeal of the newly converted: "Signor Barbaggi was frequently repeating to me, that the Corsicans inhabited a rude uncultivated country, and that they lived like Spartans. I begged leave to ask in what country he could shew me greater luxury than I had seen in his house; and I said I should certainly tell wherever I went, what tables the Corsicans kept, notwithstanding their pretensions to poverty and temperance" (303–304).

In this general context of awakening and embarrassment, Boswell moves effortlessly and inexorably to the pertinent political issues. Leaving the house where he had been repaid with kindness after thoughtlessly treating the owners as if they were servants, he tells us he was confronted by a guardsman at the Provincial Magistracy and that he was forced to be as ashamed for his country as he had been for his manners: "Upon my arrival, the captain of the guard came out, and demanded who I was? I replied 'Inglese, English.' He looked at me seriously, and then said in a tone between regret and upbraiding, '. . . The English; they were once our friends; but they are so no more.' I felt for my country, and was abashed before this honest soldier" (302).

We should like to know more than we do about the extent to which Boswell distorted or altered his original factual records in writing them up for publication in the *Account of Corsica.* Very few examples of his original notes and journal records from the tour survive for the purposes of comparison. However, the journal record for 11 October 1765 does survive, and it contains material that he deliberately altered to idealize and romanticize the account of his trip from Leghorn to Corsica. A comparison of the differences between the passage as it was published in the *Journal and Memoirs* and the original gives a good indication of the kind of changes he felt free to make for the published *Journal.*

In the *Journal and Memoirs,* the record of the passage from Leghorn is very brief. It reads only: "Though from Leghorn to Corsica, is usually but one day's sailing, there was so dead a calm that it took us two days. The first day was the most tedious. However there were two or three Corsicans aboard, and one of them played on the citra, which amused me a good deal. At sunset all the people in the ship sung the Ave Maria, with great devotion and some melody. It was pleasing to enter into the spirit of their religion, and hear them offering up their evening orisons" (294–295). Professor Pottle notes that this passage, when compared with the original journal record, illustrates Boswell's tendency to "generalize and tone down his first impressions."[8] But the difference between the two passages is greater than Pottle suggests.

The original journal entry deserves full quotation, because it is significantly different from the version in the *Account of Corsica,* and because it is important to realize the extent to which Boswell felt free to exercise the powers of omission and distortion in writing up the original factual accounts for the published tour. The original reads:

Friday, 11 October. After a few hours of sleep, was called at six by Signor Giuliano and another Corsican, who beat at my door. Was confused a little, but recollecting grand expedition, blood recovered bold circulation. Wrote Rousseau and Dempster; left also letters for Mme. de Spaen and my dear Italian lady at Siena. At eight the little boat carried me to the bark, and we set sail. The good people had waited all night for me when the wind was so good that we should have been in Corsica ere morning. This day there was little wind. I was sick a very short while and threw up a little, but felt firm nerves in comparison of myself on the passage to Holland. A Corsican played a sort of guitar or lute, and I played my flute, and so did Jacob. The bark belonged to a Corsican of Pino. He carried wine to Leghorn. He spoke English. To save himself, he had the Tuscan flag (the Emperor's), and a Leghorn shipmaster, Ignazio Gentili. I lay down in the cabin bed, but was eat up by mosquitoes and other vermin. I eat cold tongue and bread and some of the crew's rice. There were ten men aboard; two poor Corsican merchants, six Corsican sailors, the master, and a boy from Leghorn. I tried to read a little the disputes of Corsica, but could give no attention. Thought hardly any, and was content to be so. Jacob was firm and felt no sickness but wished to have a long voyage, and at night was delighted to see nothing but the sky and the sea. They laid a mattress on the provision chest, and hung a sail on the side of the bark and on four chairs, and under this tent you slept. At the Ave Maria they all

---

[8] *Yale Edition of the Private Papers,* IV, p. 151.

kneeled, and with great fervency said their evening orisons to the
Queen of Heaven. It affected you a good deal.[7]

The difference between the two passages is greater than one
simply of toning down and generalization. All personal details
are omitted and more than just the leaving out of information
of obviously peripheral importance such as the name of the shipmaster or the cargo, the literary character of the passage was
altered considerably by the omission of almost all self-reference
and self-analysis. The study of his own reactions and the careful
record of the frequent changes of mood and state of mind are
what mark the original passage as typically Boswellian. None of
the negative aspects of the trip mentioned in the original are
even hinted at in the published version—the sea sickness, the
vermin, etc. All this is compressed into the observation that the
first day was "the most tedious." In the published account Boswell retained only the record of the Corsican musician who he
tells us helped to relieve the tedium—there is no such statement
of the particular efficacy of the Corsican in the original—and
the account of the evening prayers.

In the same way that Boswell's history is not like other histories, his *Journal* is not like his other journals. In writing up
the original factual records, his propagandistic objectives caused
him to alter radically the literary character of these records to
make them project an idealized version of the Corsicans and
their life style. Instead of focusing on himself, they are made
to focus on the subject of the work—the romanticized picture of
the Corsicans. Altered as they were for publication in the
Account of Corsica, the journals have all the illusion and the
imaginative force of a personal record, and all the one-sidedness
consonant with the objective of persuasion that obtains throughout the work.

This is the literary context in which the portrait of Paoli must

---

[7] *Yale Edition of the Private Papers,* IV, pp. 139–141.

be viewed for a proper assessment of its organic relationship to the rest of the work. When critics have discussed the portrait they have sometimes noted "propaganda elements" in it[8] as if they were somehow separate and distinct from the *Account* proper, or from the portrait of Paoli itself. But the *Account* and the *Journal* function together artistically. The same kinds of alteration of the original factual records that we have just been discussing in connection with the *Journal* are practiced in the portrait of Paoli and for the same reasons: details are omitted, and descriptions and dramatizations are consistently made to project only selected impressions and to bear the weight of direct statement of the "message" of the work as well as the other representational limitations. In fact, the portrait of Paoli is not biography or biographical in the same way that either of the later portraits of Johnson are and should not be compared with them on the basis of equivalence.

Mr. Pottle quite accurately summarizes the major differences between the portrait of Paoli in the *Journal and Memoirs* and the later portraits of Johnson. He characterizes the portrait of Paoli as "Plutarchian" (emphasizing not only the direct allusions to Plutarch but the general tendency to heroicize and idealize); and he characterizes the portraits of Johnson as "Flemish" (emphasizing the great attention to detail and lifelikeness). He notes that there is suppression of detail in the *Account of Corsica* in contrast to the richness of detail in the *Life;* and that the portrait of Paoli is almost completely "onesided" to assure approbation, whereas we get Johnson "warts and all."[9] Close analysis, following Professor Pottle's lead, reveals that indeed, all of Boswell's most important dramatic and representational techniques were affected by his propagandistic motives: description, development of records of the General's

---

[8] Tinker, *Young Boswell*, pp. 110–116.
[9] Pottle, *James Boswell: The Earlier Years*, p. 363.

conversation, and dramatization of his actions or anecdotes about him.

Description of external details, especially to characterize his subject, was one of Boswell's gifts. As many of the descriptions of Johnson in the *Life* testify, he had a remarkably discerning eye for the minor detail or mannerism that was symbolic of the personality or some aspect of the personality. But we get very little specific external detail in the portrait of Paoli. There are no details that effectively particularize him. In the first description of him, the report that he had "a sensible, free, and open countenance" (315) is mere epitomization of the national virtues Boswell has been trying to establish. He also tells us that he was in his fortieth year and was dressed in green and gold. But this gives us very little when we think of it in comparison with the highly individualizing descriptive passages in the *Life* like those of Johnson, wig askew, wearing heavy gloves as he rummages through his dusty library, or attacking his dinner, the veins standing out on his forehead. Given Boswell's propagandistic motives that kind of specificity would not have been desirable: Paoli is to be a striking and convincing focal point for our attention, but not a distraction from the issues.

That Boswell was selective in choosing when to describe in full detail and when to outline or merely highlight is made clear when we compare the above description with that of the "Corsican Soldier" from the *Account*. In the latter, Boswell's eye for minute (Flemish) detail was working at full strength. He tells us:

A Corsican is armed with a gun, a pistol and a stiletto. He wears a short coat, of a very coarse dark cloth, made in the island, with waistcoat and breeches of the same, or of French or Italian cloth, especially scarlet. He has a cartridge-box or pouch for his ammunition, fixed round his middle, by a belt. Into this pouch his stiletto is stuck; and on the left side of his belt he hangs a pistol. His gun is slung across his shoulder. He wears black leather spatterdashes, and a sort of bonnet of black cloth, lined with red freeze, and ornamented on the front, with a piece of some finer stuff neatly sewed about. (210–211)

Since Boswell had an equal opportunity to observe both Paoli and uniformed Corsican soldiers, it seems clear that he chose not to describe Paoli in greater detail than he did. He was not trying to realize him in full visual detail or, as we shall see, as a complex human being with subtleties and contradictions as part of the portrait. Definition of him as a complex individual— by any means—was subordinate to the case Boswell was making for the Corsicans, and almost every word had political overtones.

Descriptions of particulars about Paoli's style of life do not particularize or characterize the private man as they do so effectively with Johnson in the *Life.* Either subtly or directly they proclaim the political "message." For example, in describing Paoli's table Boswell notes that: "He had an Italian cook who had been long in France; but he chose to have a few plain substantial dishes, avoiding every kind of luxury, and drinking no foreign wine" (317). This brief passage, down to individual words and phrases, can be explained, like many others, entirely in terms of its propagandistic function. We remember that it was particularly important that Boswell present Paoli in a manner that showed him to be both an extension of his own people and yet worthy of formal recognition by any European power. Thus he had to emphasize the fact that, "He had an Italian cook who had been long in France" (that is, he was an accomplished gentleman by Continental standards); but that like a true leader and extension of his people, and a true disciple of Rousseau's, he preferred substance and simplicity, rejecting the corrupting influence of foreign tastes. The passage tells us little, if anything, about Paoli the private individual. As always, his character is merged with the national characteristics of the Corsicans. A description of what dishes he liked or how he ate them—the

kind of information we get in such abundance about Johnson—
would have told something about the individual. But we get
none.

Again, like many in the *Journal and Memoirs,* the following
description of an aspect of Paoli's character is almost purely
informational—not about the private individual, but about his
disposition (and, by implication, the formal diplomatic posture
of the Corsicans) toward the British. Boswell writes, "He was
well acquainted with the history of Britain. He had read many
of the parliamentary debates, and had even seen a number of
the North Briton. He shewed a considerable knowledge of this
country, and often introduced anecdotes and drew comparisons
and allusions from Britain" (322). Like the descriptive passage
cited above, this really tells us very little about Paoli. Did he
like the *North Briton?* What were some of the anecdotes and
allusions that he drew? We get no value judgments—those
would betray concrete aspects of his personality—other than
the implied favorable interest in Britain. The point of the passage is precisely to convey that information and not to individualize Paoli further.

Boswell's treatment of Paoli's conversation is particularly
unlike his usual manner of dramatizing records of conversations
either in the journals or the *Life of Johnson,* and the relatively
small amount of factual record[10] he had for the sketch of Paoli
cannot be blamed for this aspect of his treatment of it. He had
about the same amount of journal record for his visit with Rousseau and less for Voltaire; but his treatment of them in his
journals is much more in keeping with what is considered his
usual dramatic technique.

In the *Journal and Memoirs* there is only the barest possible
realization of a social or dramatic context for most of Paoli's
statements. It is usually little more than "a circle of heroes," or
"the brave islanders," not named and at least partially individ-

---

[10] Pottle, *James Boswell: The Earlier Years,* p. 363.

ualized speakers. The formula Boswell uses almost exclusively is the simple, "speaking of such-and-such, he said . . . ." The quotations are usually separated by informational descriptive passages like the one cited above (as opposed to their forming any extended dramatic sequence). The subjects vary little relative to any comparable segment of the *Tour to the Hebrides* or the *Life of Johnson*. Unlike the later works, there is surprisingly little interchange dramatized between Boswell and Paoli, or between Boswell and anyone. There is very little variety of tone or mood—no "tossing and goring." Conversation on a wide variety of subjects would have dispersed his readers' attention too widely, causing them to concentrate more on details about Paoli himself and less on the purely heroic aspects of him and the specific statements he was making about the Corsicans and their cause.

We know that Boswell had the material for something different. There is evidence that he had anecdotes that reveal an earthier, spicier side of Paoli[11] that he chose to omit in the published *Journal and Memoirs*. But he includes only sayings that heroicize Paoli, or that bear directly upon the political "message" of the book. Marmoreal statements flow with great regularity: " 'Our state,' said he, 'is young, and still requires the leading strings. I am desirous that the Corsicans should be taught to walk of themselves' " (322–323); " ' . . . to accept of the highest offices under a foreign power would be to serve' " (328); " 'I defy Rome, Sparta or Thebes to show me thirty years of such patriotism as Corsica can boast' " (333).

The substance of the quotations is usually fine enough. But we get them in such high relief that they have little dramatic power beyond the force of the literal statement. They are not made focal points in universally understandable social dramas as in the *Life* where (when Johnson thunders at his best) fool-

---

[11] Pottle, *James Boswell: The Earlier Years*, p. 363.

ishness is rebuked, the air is cleared of cant, or the dignity of
man is asserted. Statements like the above in the *Journal and
Memoirs* have the simple and direct function of ennobling the
Corsicans and Paoli for the purpose of making them appear
eminently worthy of recognition and assistance by the British.

Only occasionally do we get something different. In a rare
moment that gives us a glimpse behind the heroic facade, Boswell tells us that Paoli observed to him, " 'I will never marry.
I have not the conjugal virtues. Nothing would tempt me to
marry, but a woman who should bring me an immense dowry,
with which I might assist my country' " (329). The value judgment here—the self-analysis—gives us just a hint of a particular
personality behind the paradigm. But it seems likely that it was
included because of the sentiment about the use of the dowry—
showing Paoli's singleminded devotion to his cause. And all too
often the way we see him is such that the image amounts to little
more than a statue. In fact at one point Boswell makes the direct
comparison for us. After continuing to emphasize the image of
Paoli as a man of the world and an accomplished gentleman,
Boswell asks him how he can stand to confine himself to his
own relatively uncivilized country surrounded constantly by
danger to his own person. "He replied," writes Boswell, "in one
line of Virgil:

'Vincet amor patriae laudumque immensa cupido.'
This uttered with the fine open Italian pronunciation, and the
graceful dignity of his manner, was very noble. I wished to have
a statue of him taken at that moment" (320–321). In the sense
of the relative artificiality of the passage as compared with a
dramatized conversation from the *Life,* Boswell has indeed
taken a statue of him.

However, as we have seen in the discussion of the *Account,*
as a propagandist Boswell was not subtle. The acid test as to
whether his portrayal of Paoli is a direct function of these same

propagandistic intentions ought to be greater than the evidence by implication that we have discussed above. Obligingly Boswell supplies us with just such evidence.

As it is his method throughout the work to proceed from the general impressions he wanted to make to more direct political reference, so he proceeds in the portrayal of Paoli. Toward the end of the work, Paoli is made to speak directly to the practical, political point—the designation of the Corsicans as rebels and the inaction of Great Britain. Boswell feeds him the proper question and Paoli responds with predictable eloquence: "I mentioned to him the scheme of an alliance between Great Britain and Corsica. Paoli with politeness and dignity waved the subject, by saying, 'The less assistance we have from allies, the greater our glory.' He seemed hurt by our treatment of his country. He mentioned the severe proclamation of the last peace, in which the brave islanders were called the Rebels of Corsica. He said with a conscious pride and proper feeling, 'Rebels! I did not expect that from Great Britain'" (342).

The approach is fairly sophisticated. Boswell was intelligent enough to understand that his interests did not lie simply in a castigation of Britain—that was not the way to win her sympathy. The tone of the entire work is not one of outrage but one of wonder: why won't England come to the aid of a gallant people like these? In the very next paragraph he softens Paoli's outburst and makes of it a clear statement of the *raison d'être* of the book: "He however shewed his great respect for the British nation, and I could see he wished much to be in friendship with us. When I asked him what I could possibly do in return for all this goodness to me, he replied, 'Solamente disingannate il suo corte, Only undeceive your court. Tell them what you have seen here. They will be curious to ask you'" (342–343).

The episode with Paoli closes, in fact, with a political parable. Boswell in his role as narrator tries to assuage Paoli's fears, and to speak, he hopes, for more Britons than himself: "I expressed such hopes as a man of sensibility would in my situation naturally form. He saw at least one Briton devoted to his cause. I threw out many flattering ideas of future political events, imaged the British and the Corsicans strictly united both in commerce and war, and described the blunt kindness and admiration with which the hearty, generous common people of England would treat the brave Corsicans" (343). Paoli's spirits, we are to believe, brightened at such a prospect. And then, as if out of Aesop: " 'Do you remember,' said he, 'the little people in Asia who were in danger of being oppressed by the great king of Assyria, till they addressed themselves to the Romans: and the Romans, with the noble spirit of a great and free nation, stood forth, and would not suffer the great king to destroy the little people, but made an alliance with them?'

"He made no observations upon this beautiful piece of history," write Boswell. "It was easy to see his allusion to his own nation and ours" (343).

Biographers can do many things in attempting to recreate the life or personality of another human being. Sometimes they concentrate on the history of his life, some special achievement, or perhaps his professional career. Sometimes they concentrate on their subject's personality or some particularly significant aspects of it. This of course does not begin to exhaust the possibilities. But it seems clear that Boswell, in his portrayal of Pasquale Paoli, did not have the objectives of the biographer uppermost in his mind. The biographical function of the portrait is consistently subordinated to its propagandistic function. And in literary and dramatic terms it is not, by any means, a direct antecedent of the later portraits of Johnson.

Since the discovery of the *Malahide Papers* it has been clear that Boswell had all of his most important literary and dramatic skills well before he wrote a line of the *Account of Corsica*. The fact that there are important stylistic differences between the portrait of Paoli and the later portraits of Johnson does not mean that the portrait of Paoli represents simply an early stage of Boswell's literary apprenticeship. The differences are the result of conscious artistic choices made by Boswell and indicate that he actively exercised organizational powers and was concerned with producing larger than local literary effects. He was quite capable, to contradict Stauffer's assertion, of distorting actual events to fit a preconception.

II. THE *TOUR TO THE HEBRIDES*

THERE ARE IMPORTANT differences too between Boswell's methods for developing his primary factual materials about Johnson in the *Tour* and the *Life*. What I shall suggest in this and the following chapter is that in the *Tour* Boswell seems to be primarily concerned with juxtaposing a static and essentially stereotypic image of Johnson (the public's image) and the unique and incongruous situations in which he finds him on the tour. In the *Life* he develops many of the same kinds of primary materials about Johnson quite differently because there he is primarily concerned with building a cumulative and extremely complex image of Johnson's character— his private character as well as the public's image, and one that defies many of the very stereotypes he in part depends on in the *Tour*. I shall concentrate here primarily on Boswell's development of materials involving Johnson's "singularities," appearance, and explosive temper. Boswell's development of this kind of material in the *Tour* seems to me best to demonstrate his purpose and his methods for portraying Johnson there, and affords the clearest possible contrast between his purpose and methods there and in the *Life of Johnson*. I do not mean to suggest either that this is the only kind of material he deals with in the *Tour* or that the *final* impression that the work gives is in any way reductive of Johnson. When I deal with what I consider the artistic limitations of Boswell's methods in the *Tour*, I mean limitations as compared with the portrait in the *Life;* and while I do deal with what I consider (by comparison) to be some of the more negative aspects of the portrait of Johnson in the *Tour*, I suggest that the greatest strengths of the book as well are a product of Boswell's methods for portraying Johnson there.

In a letter included in the text, Boswell wrote to Garrick from Inverness: " . . . it would not be much more wonderful to me to see St. Paul's church moving along where we now are [than it is to see Johnson]."[1] In terms of the way Boswell develops his materials about Johnson in the *Tour* he is made to seem, as the comparison to St. Paul's suggests, a venerable and much beloved public edifice in an unlikely place and not, as in the *Life of Johnson,* a human being whose character is revealed to us in all its complexity.

The most consistent source of literary pleasure in the *Tour* is the sequence of image after image of Johnson *being* the public's idea of Johnson. The summary sketch of his "form and manner" sets the stage. Placed at the beginning (unlike its counterpart in the *Life of Johnson*)[2] it provides a simplified outline of the most famous aspects of his moral, political, and literary character and his physical appearance. The aspects of his personality that are to figure most prominently are given special emphasis: ". . . he was a sincere and zealous christian, of high-church of England and monarchial principles, which he would not tamely suffer to be questioned; . . . correct, nay stern in his taste; hard to please, and easily offended, impetuous and irritable in his temper . . ." (17). And Boswell makes a point of emphasizing the unusual or even the grotesque in his appearance. "His person," he writes, "was large, robust, I may say approaching to the gigantick, and grown unwieldy from corpu-

---

[1] The text of the Tour to the Hebrides used here is Vol. V of the Hill-Powell edition of the *Life of Johnson* (Oxford, 1964). All further references will be from this edition and the page number will immediately follow the quotation. This reference is to p. 347.

[2] Boswell claimed that he used the same sketch of Johnson at the conclusion of the *Life* that he had used earlier at the beginning of the *Tour.* But in important ways the two sketches were quite different—at least in emphasis. In the *Tour,* the outlines of Johnson's moral character were summarized and simplified, and his "particularities" and the grotesque aspects of his physical appearance and infirmities were emphasized. The weighting of this kind of material is exactly reversed in the *Life of Johnson,* where Johnson's great intellectual and moral strengths are dwelt upon at length and the details about his appearance are softened and in some cases suppressed entirely.

lency. His countenance was naturally of the cast of an ancient statue, but somewhat disfigured . . ." (18). In another passage (omitted entirely from the concluding sketch in the *Life*) Boswell goes into great detail about Johnson's infirmities and "particularities": "He was now in his sixty-fourth year, and was become a little dull of hearing. . . . His head, and sometimes also his body, shook with a kind of motion like the effect of a palsy: he appeared to be frequently disturbed by cramps, or convulsive contradictions, of the nature of that distemper called *St. Vitus's dance*" (18).

Immediately on his arrival in Edinburgh Johnson begins to live up to the expectations Boswell raises. Before he can get to him, ". . . the Doctor had unluckily had a bad specimen of Scottish cleanliness. He then drank no fermented liquor. He asked to have his lemonade made sweeter; upon which the waiter, with his greasy fingers, lifted a lump of sugar, and put it into it. The Doctor, in indignation, threw it out of the window. Scott said, he was afraid he would have knocked the waiter down" (21–22). "Correct, nay stern in his taste; hard to please, impetuous and irritable in his temper," Johnson begins immediately to be the Johnson of the summary sketch, and Boswell himself is soon to feel the weight of his sarcasm: "Mr. Johnson and I walked arm-in-arm up the High-street, to my house in James's court: it was a dusky night: I could not prevent his being assailed by the evening effluvia of Edinburgh. . . . A zealous Scotsman would have wished Mr. Johnson to be without one of his five senses upon this occasion. As we marched slowly along, he grumbled in my ear, 'I smell you in the dark!' " (22–23).

The *Tour* is dotted throughout with such examples of the verbal sparks that are almost certain to fly when Johnson decides to have a good time at Scotland's expense (as with the Scotch "Bacon's wall"),[3] or when he is defending the Church of Eng-

---

[3] The *Tour to the Hebrides,* pp. 42–43.

land. In each instance Boswell singles out and invokes the appropriate aspect of his character to lend anticipatory pleasure to the outburst: "Dr. Johnson's veneration for the Hierarchy is well known," Boswell begins. "There is no wonder then, that he was affected with a strong indignation, while he beheld the ruins of religious magnificence. I happened to ask where John Knox was buried. Dr. Johnson burst out, 'I hope in the highway. I have been looking at his reformations'" (61).

Smaller anecdotes like these have a more important analogue in the *Tour*—the more elaborate contrast. The term "contrast" is Boswell's own and refers to editorial heightening of his readers' awareness of the appropriate, the unusual, or the improbable about Johnson's actions and reactions to the people and situations he encounters. Boswell continuously attempts to increase his readers' pleasure by juxtaposing Johnson's actions and the best-known aspects of his public reputation. The following is perhaps a quintessential example: "To see Dr. Johnson in any new situation is always an interesting object to me; and, as I saw him now for the first time on horseback, jaunting about at his ease in quest of pleasure and novelty, the very different occupations of his former laborious life, his admirable productions, his *London* and his *Rambler,* &c. &c. immediately presented themselves to my mind, and the contrast made a strong impression on my imagination" (132). The contrast is made between Johnson's pleasure jaunting and his reputation as a strict moralist, his former hardships and the ease of the present moment. Such essentially stereotypic characterization of Johnson excludes subtlety and possible qualification from the image in order sharply to define the bases for the contrast: moralist-jaunting, ease-hardship.

It has been suggested that in the *Tour* (and elsewhere) Boswell's powers of invention and shaping hand operate primarily on events themselves and not on the literary product.[4] But the

---

[4] The reference is to the remarks made by Professor Bronson cited above (*Introduction,* n. 12).

differences between the original journal record of this incident
and the above passage show that when Boswell wrote up his
journal for publication he consciously developed the factual
skeleton to produce this specific kind of contrast. The original
reads: "To see Mr. Johnson in any new situation is an object of
attention to me. As I saw him now for the first time ride along
just like Lord Alemoor, I thought of *London, a Poem,* of the
Rambler, of *The False Alarm;* and I cannot express the ideas
which went across my imagination."[5] This is certainly the germ
of the published version, but the key additions Boswell makes
are extremely important ones. They are: "jaunting about at his
ease in quest of pleasure and novelty, the very different occupations of his former laborious life . . . immediately presented
themselves to my mind, and the contrast made a strong impression on my imagination."[6] They point the contrast, make it
more specific, and elaborate upon it. The original passage, if left
unchanged, would have been flat and noticeably out of character
with the rest of such anecdotes in the *Tour.*

The potential for contrasts like these was great and the range
of possibilities quite broad. Sometimes it involved Johnson's

---

[5] *Boswell's Journal of a Tour to the Hebrides with Samuel Johnson,
L. L. D. Now First Published from the Original Manuscript,* ed. Frederick A. Pottle and Charles H. Bennet (New York, 1936), p. 99. In the
1964 edition of the *Tour* Professors Pottle and Bennet provide the important differences between the original and the published versions of
the *Tour* in a comprehensive series of appendices. But these differences
are not analysed formally, but are merely noted. Professor Pottle goes
much further in a more recent edition of the original *Journal* (McGraw-
Hill), dealing much more extensively with Edmund Malone's known
and possible contributions to the final version. (I discuss this in more
detail below—see note 6.) But he does not deal with the patterns and
seeming purpose behind the kinds of additions to and alterations of the
original record that I discuss here.

[6] These kinds of changes could *possibly* be attributed to Edmund
Malone but I do not think so. Professor Pottle's more recent edition of
the original *Journal* (*Boswell's Journal of a Tour to the Hebrides with
Samuel Johnson L. L. D. 1773,* ed. F. A. Pottle and Charles H. Bennet

physical size: his great bulk upon a sheltie (284–285). Sometimes the contrast was political: Johnson caught sitting under a portrait of his archenemy Wilkes (186). And a tour through the hinterlands of Scotland, still inhabited by people who "went out in the forty-five," was certain to produce some memorable scenes involving the "champion of the English Tories." Seeing Dr. Johnson salute Flora Macdonald and then, in the same house, the sight of Dr. Johnson in the bed that had once held Prince Charles, sends Boswell's imagination racing: "To see Dr. Samuel Johnson lying in that bed, in the isle of Sky, in the house of Miss Flora Macdonald, struck me with such a group of ideas as it is not easy for words to describe . . ." (186). As always, when the dramatic high point is reached, Boswell's description telescopes outward in a climactic series of phrases collecting all the relevant information together: Dr. Samuel Johnson . . . in that bed . . . in the isle of Skye . . . in the house of Flora Macdonald.

But Boswell seems fondest of such contrasts when they involve incongruity and have a hint of the humorous about them. He seems genuinely to have delighted in this mild form of irreverence to the mighty sage and a large part of the appeal of the *Tour* is the new perspective on Johnson such scenes provide. For example, he writes, "To me it was highly comick, to see the grave philosopher,—the Rambler,—toying with a Highland beauty!" (261). And more elaborately still: "To hear the grave

[New York, 1961]) deals with this question in some detail but suggests that Malone's strongest influence was that of imposing a greater degree of elegance, generality (p. xi) and decorum on the much more personal and highly specific original. The strongest criticisms of the *Tour* after its publication dealt too with such things as the inclusion of unflattering references to living persons and other such breaches of decorum. The kinds of changes (additions or omissions) I deal with here are those specifically related to the creation of certain kinds of literary effects in portraying Johnson himself. This does not seem to me to fall into the category of those elements of the book in which Malone's hand is clearly to be seen.

Dr. Samuel Johnson, 'that majestick teacher of moral and religious wisdom,' while sitting solemn in an armchair in the Isle
of Skye, talk, *ex cathedra,* of his keeping a seraglio, and ac-
knowledge that the supposition had *often* been in his thoughts,
struck me so forcibly with ludicrous contrast, that I could not
but laugh immoderately" (216). The basic contrast (moralist-
seraglio) is heightened with skill and economy. The most important elements come in a rapid-fire succession of descriptive
phrases: "The grave Dr. Samuel Johnson . . . 'that majestick
teacher . . .' while sitting solemn . . . in the Isle of Skye . . ." building to the italicized *"ex cathedra"* and *"often."* The characterizing epithet is ponderously dwelt upon, and the description of
Johnson's posture ("sitting solemn in an arm-chair") lends
comic solemnity to the force of *"ex cathedra."*

This anecdote too, when compared with the original journal
record, allows us to see Boswell's shaping hand at work on the
literary product. The original record of the portion reproduced
in the published *Tour* reads only, "To hear Mr. Johnson, while
sitting solemn in arm-chair, talk of his keeping a seraglio and
saying too, 'I have *often* thought,' was truly curious." The additions made for the published version are the following key
phrases invoking the appropriate aspects of Johnson's reputation and pointing the contrast much more elaborately: ". . . the
grave Dr. . . . 'that majestick teacher of moral and religious
wisdom,' . . . talk *ex cathedra* . . . struck me so forcibly with ludicrous contrast, that I could not but laugh immoderately."

But Boswell's concentration upon contrasts and the spectacle
Johnson provided had some less than wholly successful literary
side effects—at least when compared with his later treatment
of him in the *Life of Johnson.* The following is a good example.

On Wednesday 1 September, Boswell relates that because of
Johnson's great bulk he had to alternate horses on a particularly steep descent, and that because it was very awkward
he grumbled much and was considerably out of sorts. Boswell

tells us that he was excessively amused by the guide's methods for trying to keep Johnson in a good humor:

Hay led the horse's head, talking to Dr. Johnson as much as he could; and (having heard him, in the forenoon, express a pastoral pleasure on seeing the goats browzing) just when the Doctor was uttering his displeasure, the fellow cried, with very Highland accent, "See, such pretty goats!" Then he whistled, *whu!* and made them jump.— Little did he conceive what Dr. Johnson was. Here now was a common ignorant Highland clown imagining that he could divert, as one does a child,—*Dr. Samuel Johnson!*—The ludicrousness, absurdity, and extraordinary contrast between what the fellow fancied, and the reality, was truly comick. (144)

Though much about this passage is typical of Boswell at his best, it is not especially flattering to Johnson. Neither the picture (Johnson in a bad mood), nor the contrast (the great Dr. Johnson patronized by the foolish rustic) ennobles Johnson. All that it really shows is that the guide was foolish in thinking that he could pacify Johnson so simply. Boswell does not elaborate here on "what Dr. Johnson was," that the guide should have known better; nor does he make any effort to qualify the picture of a grumbling Johnson besieged by a foolish peasant guide. It is a funny picture and certainly not one that degrades Johnson in any way—our sympathies are with him from the start. It has the appeal shared by all anecdotes that humanize public or historically important figures by showing them to be mortal and occasionally fallible like the rest of us. But clearly, the "contrast" that Boswell points up is the sole object of its telling. Unlike the treatment of similar incidents in the *Life,* it is not made the means of revealing and developing a greater aspect of Johnson's character.

Another good example of this kind of scene is the meeting with the Reverend Hector M'Lean, at which the two gentlemen carry on simultaneous but different conversations because both are hard of hearing. "It was curious to see him and Dr. Johnson together," writes Boswell:

Neither of them heard very distinctly; so each of them talked in his own way, and at the same time. Mr. M'Lean said, he had a confutation of Bayle, by Leibnitz.—*Johnson.* "A confutation of Bayle, sir! What part of Bayle do you mean? The greatest part of his writings is not confutable: it is historical and critical."—Mr. M'Lean said, "the irreligious part;" and proceeded to talk of Leibnitz's controversy with Clarke, calling Leibnitz a great man.—*Johnson.* "Why sir, Leibnitz persisted in affirming that Newton called space *sensorium numinis,* notwithstanding he was corrected, and desired to observe that Newton's words were QUASI *sensorium numinis.* No, sir; Leibnitz was as paltry a fellow as I know. Out of respect to Queen Caroline, who patronised him, Clarke treated him too well."

During the time that Dr. Johnson was thus going on, the old minister was standing with his back to the fire, cresting up erect, pulling down the front of his periwig, and talking what a great man Leibnitz was. To give an idea of the scene, would require a page with two columns; but it ought rather to be represented by two good players. (287–288)

Even without the double columns or players, the scene is made genuinely comic and is masterfully dramatized. The picture of Johnson "going on" while at the same moment the old minister bobs birdlike on his own declamatory voyage (cresting up erect, pulling down the front of his periwig) animates the scene to comic perfection. Yet in his treatment of it Boswell clearly does not aspire to more than simply the essentially comic aspects of this image of the two aging combatants arguing simultaneously because they are hard of hearing. The scene derives most of its interest bcause Samuel Johnson was one of the participants. (Consider the diminution of interest or comedy if this same incident, between two other parties, had merely been observed by Johnson and Boswell.) Developed in this way it is appropriate in the *Tour* because Johnson's deafness causes him, though unaware, to act a part quite different from that in which we are accustomed to thinking of him: usually the dominant and controlling force in any conversation, it is a rare sight indeed to see him (comically) ineffectual in argument. That is

precisely why it is developed thus in the *Tour* and why it is not
further qualified or elaborated upon.

In general, because Boswell's literary objectives do not extend
significantly beyond the interest to be generated by the sequence
of images of Johnson doing the improbable or the unusual there
are a number of aspects of his treatment of him that are of questionable value or effectiveness. For example, the tendency towards stereotypic characterizations of Johnson—a direct function of the mode of contrast discussed above—has some potentially negative side effects. Johnson is termed variously "the
mighty sage," the Rambler," "the famed moralist," "the famous
editor of Shakespeare," the "champion of the English Tories,"
"our great lexicographer," the "majestick teacher of moral and
religious wisdom," and so on. Such epithets keep the bold and
simplified outlines of his character and history before Boswell's
readers. But because they are neither challenged nor systematically qualified (as they are in the *Life*) they allow no further
complexity to enter into the contrasts. In the *Tour* Johnson is
characterized, to a great extent, simply by what he has done:
"our great lexicographer," "the Rambler," and so forth. The
picture is essentially static. Though all of these familiar epithets
are used throughout the *Life,* there the primary emphasis is
upon what he *was* (contrary to popular belief) and how his
achievements are explainable and even take on greater significance in the light of his character. His actions are consistently
developed to reveal and interpret his character in the *Life;* but
the *Tour* was never intended to examine him so closely. And
if the epithets used to characterize Johnson in the *Tour* simplify
the image of his character, the metaphors used to describe him
verge at times on the reductive. To heighten contrasts they play
predominantly upon his size (both intellectual and physical),
especially on his ponderosity and unwieldiness. This note is
struck clearly at the beginning of the work, when he is figur-
atively given the status of a great barge to emphasize the diffi-

culties in getting the tour under way: "I knew that, if he were once launched from the metropolis, he would go forward very well; and I got our common friends there to assist in setting him afloat" (14); "With such propitious convoys did he proceed to my native city" (16).

Metaphors that contrast Johnson's "size" with his environment or antagonists are the building blocks of the descriptive writing in the *Tour:* "He stalked," Boswell tells us, "like a giant among the thistles and nettles"; (we have seen him on a sheltie); his conversational powers are likened to the "arms of Goliath"; the strength of his intellect, conventionally enough, to that of the "lofty oak." But sometimes it is questionable, I think, whether or not Johnson has been complimented when we think about the figurative parallel. "So great a mind as his cannot be moved by inferior objects," writes Boswell; "an elephant does not run and skip like lesser animals." Because Johnson's "form and manner" are dwelt upon so consistently in the *Tour,* Boswell's choice of this kind of elephant-skipping comic image cannot help invoking his other references to Johnson's physical size. Later, Boswell wrote, "He appears to me like a great mill, into which a subject is thrown to be ground." Whether or not elephants and grist mills had a positive or heroic status in the eighteenth century that has been lost in the intervening years, the comparison is clearly intended more to add to the *spectacle* of Johnson in the Hebrides than to enlarge or ennoble him.

The following is a particularly good example of the somewhat double-edged nature of this kind of figurative representation of Johnson in the *Tour*—intended more to heighten the spectacle or the contrast than to suggest (as in the *Life*) his complexity and greatness. "I was elated," writes Boswell, "by the thought of having been able to entice such a man to this remote part of the world. A ludicrous, yet just, image presented itself to my mind, which I expressed to the company. I compared myself to a dog who has got hold of a large piece of meat, and runs away to a corner, where he may devour it in peace, without any fear of others taking it from him. 'In London, Reynolds, Beauclerk, and all of them, are contending who shall enjoy Dr. Johnson's conversation. We are feasting on it, undisturbed, at Denvegan' " (215).

This image is designed, I think, to reinforce the sense of the improbability of Johnson's being in the Hebrides and to heighten the vicarious sense of the snugness of possession of him there. The light, almost mischievous tone of the passage is in keeping with the general comic lightness and controlled irreverence that characterize much that is most delightful in the work. It is in keeping too with the tendency toward simplification of the images of Johnson, the stereotypicization of his "form and manner" for the purpose of imaginative contrast. But for the moment too it makes him no more than a valuable "thing" that has been run away with: "a large piece of meat." We are to respond, of course, not only to the specific visual image but to the sense of it. But metaphor in the *Life* has a much different and a much more important role. The famous comparison of Johnson's battle with his religious doubts to that of a gladiator's in the Coliseum ("... he drove them back into their dens; but not killing them, they were still assailing him." [II, 106]) makes both an acute analysis of a serious problem of Johnson's and yet makes of him an heroic gladiator of the spirit. There is no real analogue of this kind of complex analytical metaphor in the *Tour*.

Again, because the spectacle provided by Johnson in the Hebrides—the odd or the ludicrous in particular—is made the basis of so many of the contrasts in the *Tour,* Boswell seems to have felt much freer to introduce and to elaborate upon Johnson's peculiarities and physical infirmities. The *Life,* of course, is filled with descriptions of Johnson's particularities and infirmities. But whenever we are given them in concentrated form, they are almost always qualified in such a way that while they humanize him and add complexity to the portrait, they do not diminish him. In the *Tour,* Johnson's oddities or "particularities" are seldom given any greater significance than the local interest or amusement in catching Johnson in deshabille.

The *Tour* is dotted with single instances of Johnson's "particularities": Johnson's "rolling" in the Advocates' Library, his unusual night cap, and so on. But Boswell is not really in control of all such material in the way he genuinely is in the *Life,* and he has no consistent policy for its artistic development. At one point he even catalogues Johnson's peculiarities, taking a sort of inventory without comment or analysis (306). It is simply a list of inherently interesting oddities about a famous man. In the *Life* Boswell much more consistently qualifies them and generalizes them to a greater aspect of Johnson's character. If the veins stood out on his forehead as he attacked his dinner, it was because in everything he did, "He could practice abstinence but not temperance." And (as I shall discuss in considerable detail in the following chapter), in the *Life* Boswell repeatedly turns episodes involving Johnson's oddities into powerful images of his greatness in spite of his physical defects or "peculiarities." He makes them a foil for Johnson's greatest strengths. His policy in the *Life* is never to hide Johnson's particularities; but he develops such material there in ways that only increase our admiration for Johnson—usually—because of a sense of hardships overcome or our admiration at his mental and spiritual superiority to his own eccentricities. There is no consistent attempt in the *Tour* to develop such material in this manner, because it is enough there to show Johnson in action: the odder the better.

Besides Johnson's particularities, Boswell is more random in his introduction of instances of Johnson's physical infirmities, even of the pettiest kinds, in the *Tour.* For example, when Johnson's deafness bothers him it is merely recorded, or made the basis of a comic scene like that with Mr. M'Lean; when he falls it is noted; when he is sick it is noted. And sometimes, Boswell's portrayal of him verges on the ungenerous. Once, when the country became especially rugged, Boswell tells us that at a particularly treacherous point, "there was a steep declivity on his left, to which he was so near, that there was not room for him to dismount in the usual way. He tried to alight on the other side, as if he had been a *young buck* indeed, but in the attempt he fell at his length upon the ground . . ." (206–207). This kind of anecdote of course emphasizes the difficulties a man of Johnson's age and size must have faced on such a journey. But the emphasis (the words "young buck" were italicized in the *Tour*) on Johnson's age by means of contrasting his abilities with those of a younger and more agile man is gratuitously unflattering.

Sometimes Johnson's many infirmities even become the subject of more extended discussion. ". . . I must take some merit," writes Boswell, "from my assiduous attention to him, and from my contriving that he shall be easy wherever he goes, that he shall not be asked twice to eat or drink any thing, (which always disgusts him,) that he shall be provided with water at his meals, and many such little things, which, if not attended to, would fret him" (264). In emphasizing Johnson's age, temper, and physical disabilities in this manner, Boswell reduces his stature momentarily in a way that he never allows to happen in the *Life of Johnson*. Again, this is not to pretend to assert that Boswell does not deal with this kind of material in the *Life,* but to suggest instead that because his literary objective in the portrayal of Johnson is different there he develops such materials in a different way.

The lines immediately following the above quoted passage provide a good beginning for an examination of what is, if the paradox may be entertained, both the most delightful and at times the most potentially reductive element in Boswell's treatment of Johnson in the *Tour to the Hebrides:* his portrayal of himself in his role as narrator. Following the above description of the "fussing" he had to do to keep Johnson in good humor, Boswell writes, "I also may be allowed to claim some merit in leading the conversation: I do not mean leading, as in an orchestra, by playing the first fiddle; but leading as one does a witness,—starting topicks and making him pursue them" (264). In some senses the *Tour* works as well as it does precisely because it is Boswell who is our guide to the spectacle of Johnson's adventures in the Hebrides, pointing contrasts to enrich our vicarious participation in his activities, leading him into situations that might never have occurred otherwise, and into "Johnson-isms" that might never have been uttered. But more than this, and quite different from his treatment of himself in the *Life of Johnson,* Boswell, in his role as narrator in the *Tour,* assumes a familiarity and an equality with Johnson that would have jarred seriously in the *Life.* This greater degree of familiarity leads him into occasional censorship and undercutting of Johnson in the *Tour* that, in terms of tone and directness, have no analogue in the *Life.*

We remember that Boswell laughs at the rude Highland guide for thinking that he could divert Dr. Johnson as one does a child. But he himself talks about doing almost the same thing at the beginning of the *Tour.* Speaking of the general prejudice of the English against the Scotch (which he made much of in Johnson's case throughout the *Tour*) and how he regards it, Boswell observes, ". . . when I humour any of them in an outrageous contempt of Scotland, I fairly own I treat them as children. And thus I have, at some moments, found myself obliged to treat even Dr. Johnson" (20). Calmly discussing the treatment of Johnson as a child would be unthinkable in the *Life of Johnson,* where Boswell, though he often disagrees with Johnson, always does so with a cautious and respectful deference. Often in the *Tour,* in keeping with this sometimes tone of complacent equality with his subject, he not only feels free to suggest management of him, as in the above instance, but to admonish or censor his actions, sometimes sharply. For example, when Johnson, talking for victory, teases Boswell about his relation to the Douglas Cause—an episode in Boswell's life about which he felt very proud and very strongly—Boswell flatly announces: "He roused my zeal so much, that I took the liberty to tell him he knew nothing of the cause; which I do most seriously believe was the case" (362). Anyone familiar with the *Life of Johnson* can sense the difference between this suggestion that Johnson doesn't know what he is talking about and the ways that his more outrageous talkings for victory are consistently smoothed over or even made to seem admirable.

To the extent that this is a negative factor in the *Tour* the effect of this kind of treatment is more serious as a cumulative factor than it is in any but the most painful single incidents. It is the relative frequency of such treatment by Boswell that distinguishes this aspect of the *Tour* from its counterpart in the *Life*. Small incidents of this nature occur repeatedly in the *Tour*, and the total pattern has at least a potentially limiting effect on our overall response to Johnson. It is perhaps the pattern of casual rebuttals and censorship that is the most damaging of all, for it is a form of apologizing for Johnson: "I saw Mr. Riddoch did not please him," writes Boswell. "He said to me afterwards, 'Sir, he has no vigour in his talk.' But my friend should have considered that he himself was not in good humour; so that it was not easy to talk to his satisfaction."

Besides this general irreverence, Boswell also includes in the *Tour* incidents that are more unrelievedly painful in human terms than anything he includes in the *Life*. For example, when Johnson is especially irritable with him, Boswell records the following anecdote: "Dr. Johnson was displeased at my bustling, and walking quickly up and down. He said, 'It does not hasten us a bit. It is getting on horseback in a ship. All boys do it; and you are longer a boy than others.' He himself has no alertness, or whatever it may be called; so he may dislike it, as *Oderunt hilarem tristes*" (307–308).

There are two remarks here that are more spiteful and more serious in human terms than is usually the case in either the *Tour* or the *Life*—one by Johnson and one by Boswell. Johnson's irritable directness is more caustic than usual when he goes beyond confronting Boswell with his adolescent behavior and generalizes it to a fact of his character ("and you are longer a boy than others"). It is an accusation which we know, and Johnson knew, to be tragically true; it is attacking Boswell for something that, unfortunately, was not in his power to amend—certainly a very human thing to do, but not something we are permitted to see Johnson do very often. Boswell's response is equally spiteful, and has the added element of pettiness in its having been written up later rather than being delivered on the spot. He excuses himself by invoking Horace ("he may dislike it, as 'gloomy men hate the man who is gay'") in a way that, in pointing up his and Johnson's differing temperaments, invokes also, I think, the difference in their ages ("he himself has no alertness"). If other examples of this kind of situation in the *Life* can be considered precedents, the scene would probably have been reduced there to the witty and typically Johnsonian comic simile: "It is getting on horseback in a ship." The following remark might well have been omitted or only alluded to; because, while Johnson is sometimes shown to be extremely violent in the *Life* ("Don't let us meet again tonight!"), he is never shown to cause pain intentionally, without extreme justification and elaborate qualification. In general in the *Life* Boswell does not dramatize Johnson's more questionable outbursts but records their having happened in summary fashion. When he does dramatize an explosion, it is invariably made to redound to the greater glory of Johnson. In the *Tour to the Hebrides* Boswell does not seem to have any consistent policy for developing such incidents beyond the fact of the spectacle they afford.

They are of interest primarily to the extent that they constitute an example of that particular aspect of Johnson's personality (an aspect of his personality that he goes to great lengths to qualify and even to disprove in the *Life of Johnson*). This is not to suggest that they do not, for the most part, have inherent interest and often very great comic power, but only that they are never actively developed in such a way as to ennoble or enlarge the image of Johnson's character and personality in the way that characterizes the treatment of such material in the *Life*.

At their best, episodes involving Johnson's temper fit in perfectly with the general scheme of the *Tour*. Boswell dwells heavily throughout upon select aspects of Johnson's irascibility to increase his readers' anticipation of the inevitable and delightful moments of "combat." Johnson's Scotch prejudice, his veneration for the Church of England, and his quarrel with the authenticity of the poems of Ossian alone provide many delicious instances of his being his well-known, combustible self. One of Boswell's most effective techniques is to bring his readers tantalizingly near the brink of disaster and then to save the situation before matters can become serious or painful.[7] But sometimes the storm really does break, and Boswell makes no particular effort to handle such episodes with the reserve and circumspection that characterize the treatment of similar situations in the *Life*. In a discussion about David Hume early in the *Tour,* Boswell writes that, in the heat of argument, Johnson "added *something much too rough,* both as to Mr. Hume's head and heart, which I suppress. Violence is, in my opinion, not suitable to the Christian cause. Besides, I always lived on good terms with Mr. Hume . . ." (30).

Boswell doesn't tell us what exactly Johnson said. But instead of playing the whole matter down, he emphasizes its excess,

---

[7] A good example of this "going to the brink of war" and retreating safely is the early skirmish in the Advocates' Library in Edinburgh before leaving on the actual tour. *Tour,* pp. 40–41.

whatever it was, and registers his disapproval. This kind of censoriousness, especially of the ethics of Johnson's Christianity, would never have occurred in the *Life*. Boswell never presumes to criticize directly Johnson's actions there, especially anything done in the name of his religion. In the *Life,* if we may hypothesize, there would have been some kind of qualification, perhaps emphasis on the strength and sincerity of Johnson's piety leading to his *perhaps* too rigorous zeal in its defense. In this passage, however, nothing is said of Johnson except the admonition about the unsuitability of violence to the Christian cause. The rest of the episode consists of a long explanation of Boswell's own differences with Hume's position. Like the rather more serious fight between Boswell's father and Johnson at the end of the *Tour* or Johnson's outburst above ("you are longer a boy than others"), Boswell does not seem to have a policy for dealing with such material other than its inclusion if it occurred and its development as part of the spectacle of Johnson being the Johnson of the introductory sketch.

In the *Life* Boswell transcends the mode of representing Johnson in the *Tour* which I have characterized here as static and stereotypic. This is not to suggest that the *Tour* is less than a unique and delightful literary achievement, or that along with the comedy and the "contrasts" there is not much in it that is touching and highly serious. I have chosen these elements because they seem to me best to exemplify Boswell's mode of dramatizing his primary factual material in the work and because they afford a particularly clear contrast with his treatment of similar kinds of primary material in the *Life*. While I have emphasized the limitations of some of Boswell's methods I have tried to suggest that the greatest strength of the *Tour* as well lies in precisely the picture it affords of Johnson being Johnson in such an incongruous environment. But in the *Tour,* Boswell does not attempt to deal with Johnson in terms that go beyond the popular image of his "form and manner" to the complexity of the man. Most importantly, he does not attempt actively to *interpret* his character. In the *Life*, he goes beneath and beyond this popular image to the man himself in all his complexity and in all his great intellectual and moral strength. Direct quotation of Johnson with little or no embellishment of course sounds the same in both works because the inherent greatness of the source is the same. But in those cases (and they are many) where Boswell exercises his powers to omit or include, to select and interpret, and selectively to dramatize episodes and conversations in a context of his own creation, we are given different kinds of portraits of Johnson in the *Tour to the Hebrides* and the *Life of Johnson*.

III. THE *LIFE OF JOHNSON*

Boswell's special achievement in the *Life of Johnson* is not directly anticipated by the *Tour to Hebrides*. The specific nature and the extent of his conscious artistry in the *Life* are best understood when the portrait of Johnson there is viewed in *contrast* to the earlier work and not as a logical stylistic outgrowth of it. From exactly the same kinds of primary factual materials that Boswell developed to produce essentially comic effects and "contrasts" in the *Tour* he built in the *Life* some of the most powerful images of Johnson's greatest personal strengths, and a complex and heroic image of his character. Quite in accord with the work already done by Professors Rader and Waingrow, the differences between the two portraits show that the portrait of Johnson in the *Life* is a creation in every sense of the term that can properly be applied to a factual work.

In an elaborate indictment of Mrs. Piozzi in the text of the *Life* for what he considers a negative and unsympathetic representation of Johnson, Boswell makes, by implication, a formal policy statement about his own methods for dealing with all of his materials about Johnson in the work. (Marshall Waingrow concurs in regarding it as a valid statement of artistic intention.)[1] Of Mrs. Piozzi Boswell warns us:

As a sincere friend of the great man whose Life I am writing, I think it necessary to guard my readers against the mistaken notion of Dr. Johnson's character, which this lady's "Anecdotes" of him suggest; for from the very nature and form of her book, it "lends deception lighter wings to fly."

"Let it be remembered," (says an eminent critick, [Malone])

---

[1] Waingrow, citing this attack by Boswell upon Mrs. Piozzi's *Anecdotes,* observes that: "It is in his animadversions upon the *Anecdotes,* if anywhere, that something approaching a statement of principle is to be found." Waingrow, p. xliv.

"that she has comprised in a small volume all that she could recollect of Dr. Johnson in *twenty years,* during which period, doubtless, some severe things were said by him; and they who read the book in *two hours,* naturally enough suppose that his whole conversation was of this complexion. But the fact is, I have been often in his company, and never *once* heard him say a severe thing to any one; and many others can attest the same. When he did say a severe thing, it was generally extorted by ignorance pretending to knowledge, or by extreme vanity or affectation."[2]

Boswell then takes an example from Mrs. Piozzi's text which he juxtaposes with his own evaluative dramatization of the same anecdote. A careful examination of the way in which he artistically remedies Mrs. Piozzi's "errors" provides, I think, an insight into one of the most important facts about Boswell's portrayal of Johnson in the *Life.* Mrs. Piozzi's version reads: " 'That natural roughness of his [Johnson's] manner so often mentioned, would, notwithstanding the regularity of his notions, burst through them all from time to time; and he once bade a very celebrated lady, who praised him with too much zeal perhaps, or perhaps too strong an emphasis, (which always offended him,) consider what her flattery was worth, before she choaked *him* with it' " (IV, 341). Boswell's own, "true" version of the same anecdote reads as follows:

The person thus represented as being harshly treated, though a very celebrated lady, [Hannah More] was *then* just come to London from an obscure situation in the country. At Sir Joshua Reynolds's one evening, she met Dr. Johnson. She very soon began to pay her court to him in the most fulsome strain. "Spare me, I beseech you, dear Madam," was his reply. She still *laid it on.* "Pray, Madam, let us have no more of this;" he rejoined. Not paying any attention to these warnings, she continued still her eulogy. At length, provoked by this indelicate and *vain* obtrusion of compliment, he exclaimed, "Dearest

---

[2] This and all further reference to the *Life* will be to the Hill-Powell edition of the *Life of Johnson.* All future reference will be by volume and page number at the time of the quotation. This reference is to IV, pp. 340–342.

lady, consider with yourself what your flattery is worth, before you
bestow it so freely." (IV, 341)

"How different," says Boswell, "does this story appear, when
accompanied with all these circumstances which really belong
to it . . . ." But in some senses the most important "circumstances" in this anecdote were clearly open to interpretation, and
the difference between the way the story was developed by each
biographer is greater than simply the inclusion or omission of
facts. The major difference between these two accounts is not
one of concrete facts but one of interpretation of what the "facts"
show us about Johnson; and for Boswell the most important
"truth" that Mrs. Piozzi has omitted in her account is a truth
about Johnson's character.

In dramatizing her version of this incident, Mrs. Piozzi takes
"that natural roughness . . . [that] notwithstanding the regularity of his notions, burst through them all from time to time,"
to be the basic fact about Johnson's character which is demonstrated. In accord with this view of the significance of the incident as it is symbolic of a greater aspect of Johnson's personality,
she develops it in a way that makes the injured lady a sympathetic figure and Johnson a temperamental and perhaps incon-
siderate one. In her version the lady *perhaps* praised him too
much, and with *perhaps* too strong an emphasis. But Mrs.
Piozzi chooses not to dramatize her praises and her emphasis.
By dramatizing only Johnson's outburst she gives all the dramatic force in the scene to the image of Johnson's moment of
anger—the moment when the natural roughness bursts forth.

Boswell's development of the incident includes exactly the
same factual skeleton—that a lady overpraised Johnson and at
last he lost patience with her—but in dramatic terms he exactly
reverses Mrs. Piozzi's evaluative structuring of the scene. The
point he sees the incident as making is stated clearly in the
paragraph that precedes the two examples: "When he did say

a severe thing, it was generally extorted by ignorance pretending to knowledge, or by extreme vanity or affectation." He develops the scene to make us feel strongly that Johnson's retort was extorted from him by extreme vanity and affectation. Reversing Mrs. Piozzi's method, he dramatizes Hannah More's attentions to Johnson in a way that insures that we view them as vain and affected. She begins to pay her court to Johnson "in the most fulsome strain." Boswell dramatizes Johnson's increasingly direct attempts to warn her off. But "she still *laid it on*." For, "not paying any attention to these warnings, she continued still her eulogy." At last, as we were prepared, a strong retort is extorted from Johnson by "this indelicate and *vain* obtrusion of compliment." Whatever the true facts of the matter, in Boswell's version all the dramatic power is concentrated in the image of the obnoxious idolator and to a lesser degree in Johnson's attempts to head off the trouble.

For our purposes here, the significance of the difference between Mrs. Piozzi's and Boswell's evaluative dramatizations of the same incident is not that it should cause us to exclaim, like jesting Pilate, "What is truth?" but that it should make us aware of the extent to which purely artistic choices (to dramatize or not to dramatize) shape our response to "facts" as well as to "fiction," and the extent to which the making of such choices by a biographer *means,* in effect, interpretation. This would be stating the obvious except for the fact that it is precisely these kinds of interpretive powers that have been consistently denied to Boswell, as if he were a kind of thoughtless artificer marvelously adept at dramatizing objective facts.

The extent to which Boswell practiced this kind of selective and interpretive dramatization of his materials in the *Life* is made especially clear when we compare his treatment of just those aspects of Johnson's character and appearance that he turned most often to comedy and contrast in the *Tour.* Professor Waingrow's intensive work with Boswell's materials about Johnson obtained by correspondence reveals a curious fact regarding his treatment of Johnson's appearance, particularities, temper, and other weaknesses. There is a strange mixture of suppression yet accuracy, sugar-coating but with an essential honesty:

> His indolence, his oddities and asperity of manner, his excesses in eating and drinking, his profanity and bawdy, his sexual lapses, his intellectual narrowness and prejudice, his use of drugs, his insanity— all of these subjects appear among the unused sources, and seem to compose themselves into a pattern of suppression. Yet it is an equally demonstrable fact that all of these subjects are admitted to the published work in one form or another. Whatever construction Boswell may have put upon Johnson's weaknesses, it cannot be said that he concealed either the fact or the issue.[3]

Boswell's ability in the *Life* to represent vividly the strong features of Johnson's appearance, his oddities, and his sometimes volcanic excesses of temper and yet build them into foils for some of his greatest personal strengths is one of the most important differences between his treatment of Johnson in the *Life* and the *Tour.*

Elaborate arguments are not needed to demonstrate that it was easier for Boswell to dramatize Johnson's sometimes strange or uncouth appearance, or his "singularities" in such a way as to make them laughable or lovable than it was to make them the bases for respect and admiration. The kind of cruel caricature to which the bold outlines of his character and appearance lent themselves is made clear enough in the poem about him by a Mr. Cuthbert Shaw, part of which Boswell includes in the text of the *Life* itself. Wrote Shaw:

> Here Johnson comes,—unblest with outward grace,
> His rigid morals stamp'd upon his face.
> While strong conceptions struggle in his brain;
> (For even Wit is brought to bed with pain:)

---

[3] Waingrow, p. xxxvi.

To view him, porters with their loads would rest,
And babes cling frighted to the nurse's breast.
With looks convuls'd, he roars in pompous strain,
And like an angry lion, shakes his mane.
The Nine, with terror struck, who ne'er had seen,
Aught human with so horrible a mien,
Debating whether they should stay or run,
Virtue steps forth, and claims him for her son.
. . . . (II, 31–32)

In describing Johnson's appearance and dramatizing his particularities this is the kind of image (there had been other such
poems in the century)⁴ that Boswell risks invoking. In the *Tour*
he had dramatized such material with the primary intention
of evoking sympathetic laughter at the sight, for instance, of
the great bulk on the tiny sheltie or the giant "stalking among
the thistles and nettles." In the *Life,* however, while preserving
all the convincing true-to-life vividness of Johnson's appearance,
he consistently counterbalances it or makes it a focal point
which sets off his essential strength. A deceptively simple and
very good example of the way he does this is the following
anecdote about Johnson's peculiar method of walking. Boswell
tells us:

On Monday, March 19, I arrived in London, and on Tuesday, the

⁴ Among the more notable poems ridiculing some aspect of Johnson's
appearance, character, etc., were Charles Churchill's "The Ghost," sat-
irizing his supposed credulity about the Cock Lane Ghost, and regrettably
some poems by Boswell himself. For example, he and Wilkes wrote a
scurrilous poem entitled, "Ode by Dr. Johnson to Mrs. Thrale on their
Supposed Upcoming Nuptials," which played heavily upon Johnson's
ponderosity. A stanza which Boswell even included in the *Life* (without
mentioning his own part in it) reads as follows:

> *Cervisial coctor's viduate* dame
> *Opin'st* thou this gigantick frame,
> *Procumbing* at thy shrine:
> Shall, *catenated* by thy charms,
> A captive in thy *ambient* arms
> *Perennially* be thine? (IV, 387)

20th, met him in Fleet-street, walking, or rather indeed moving along; for his peculiar march is thus described in a very just and picturesque manner, in a short Life of him published very soon after his death:—"When he walked the streets, what with the constant roll of his head, and the concomitant motion of his body, he appeared to make his way by that motion, independent of his feet." That he was often much stared at while he advanced in this manner, may easily be believed; but it was not safe to make sport of one so robust as he was. Mr. Langton saw him one day, in a fit of absence, by a sudden start, drive the load off a porter's back, and walk forward briskly, without being conscious of what he had done. The porter was very angry, but stood still, and eyed the huge figure with much earnestness, till he was satisfied that his wisest course was to be quiet, and take up his burthen again. (IV, 71–72)

Johnson's characteristic walk is carefully and vividly described here, but it is deftly turned into an image of a very different kind. In defiance of strict chronology, Boswell links the initial description of Johnson's manner of walking with an anecdote from another period of his life which puts his awkward gait in a sharply different perspective: "That he was often much stared at . . . may easily be believed; but it was not safe to make sport of one so robust as he was." Like many in the *Life,* the incident with the porter is one which Boswell did not see himself. But he dramatizes it fully, down to Johnson's brisk gait and the succession of (imagined) thoughts in the porter's mind. The initial image of Johnson's awkward gait is turned round to an image of his great physical strength that defied presumptuous stares and by its very presence kept rudeness in its place. When the full anecdote is told we share, I think, the porter's involuntary tribute to the strength and "presence" of Johnson: "The porter was very angry, but stood still, and eyed the huge figure with much earnestness, till he was satisfied that his wisest course was to be quiet, and take up his burthen again."

The most common and perhaps the most dramatically impressive of Boswell's techniques for dealing with Johnson's appearance and particularities (while representing them in all their vividness) is to make them formally (and not implicitly) the foil for his great intellectual powers. The most succinct statement of what this technique involves can be found in an anecdote from the *Life* of a slightly different kind. Speaking of a portrait of Johnson originally in Beauclerk's possession, Boswell tells us: "On the frame of his portrait, Mr. Beauclerk had inscribed,

> ' . . . . *Ingenium ingens*
> *Inculto latet hoc sub corpore.*' " (IV, 180–181)

Wickham's translation of the quote from Horace that Beauclerk had inscribed on the painting reads, "Under that uncouth outside are hidden vast gifts of mind." This is exactly what Boswell so frequently dramatizes Johnson in all his ungainliness in order to show. He was writing for contemporary readers as well as for posterity and had nothing to gain by suppressing such material. He chose instead (as Johnson did in his own life) not to attempt to hide or apologize for the "uncouth outside" but instead to dazzle and surprise us with the "vast gifts of mind" concealed beneath it and all the more remarkable when seen in contrast with it.

The Hogarth episode is the paradigm for the development of all such materials. (The anecdote is Hogarth's, but the dramatization of it is Boswell's own.)

While he [Hogarth] was talking, he perceived a person standing at a window in the room, shaking his head, and rolling himself about in a strange ridiculous manner. He had concluded that he was an ideot, whom his relations had put under the care of Mr. Richardson, as a very good man. To his great surprize, however, this figure stalked forwards to where he and Mr. Richardson were sitting, and all at once took up the argument, ... he displayed such a power of eloquence, that Hogarth looked at him with astonishment, and actually imagined that this ideot had been at the moment inspired. (I, 146–147)

Boswell vividly dramatizes Johnson's "particularities" here but makes them a foil for his greatness of intellect. Although he obviously knew who the "person" was all along, he recreates the scene entirely from Hogarth's point of view. It is told by a third person, but not omniscient author and like Hogarth we see only "a person . . . shaking his head, and rolling himself about in a strange ridiculous manner." The "figure" then "stalked forwards to where he and Mr. Richardson were sitting," and Johnson's eloquence explodes upon us as it did upon Hogarth. By handling it in this way Boswell enables us, for a moment, to understand the surprise that Hogarth must have felt when this assumed idiot began a brilliant attack on George the Second in the familiar Johnsonian manner.

This kind of situation occurs repeatedly in the *Life,* permitting convincing and dramatically effective physical representations of Johnson which, while they make him all the more astounding and individualize and particularize him, do not jeopardize his essential dignity or diminish his stature. Langton's first meeting with him is another good example of the type. Mr. Langton, Boswell tells us:

... was exceedingly surprized when the sage first appeared. He had not received the smallest intimation of his figure, dress, or manner. From perusing his writings, he fancied he should see a decent, well-drest, in short, a remarkably decorous philosopher. Instead of which, down from his bed-chamber, about noon, came, as newly risen, a huge uncouth figure, with a little dark wig which scarcely covered his head, and his clothes hanging loose about him. But his conversation was so rich, so animated, and so forcible, and his religious and political notions so congenial with those in which Mr. Langton had been educated, that he conceived for him that veneration and attachment which he ever preserved. (I, 247–248)

There is a "contrast" here that is touched upon so deftly that its potentially ludicrous aspects are not realized at all. That is the contrast between Johnson's reputation and his actual appearance. Boswell makes the contrast, and allows us, along with Langton, to enjoy the very real pleasure of seeing the great man as he "really lived" and not as we might have imagined him from his works. But he does not heighten or embellish this aspect of it. Instead he goes on to explain how Langton's initial reaction was completely overthrown by the power of Johnson's mind as revealed in his conversation. As he did in the Hogarth episode, Boswell dramatizes the scene from Langton's point of view. He, of course, knows who it is that is coming down the stairs. But, like Langton, for the moment we see only, "a huge uncouth figure, with a little dark wig which scarcely covered his head." And then, any potentially reductive aspects of this delightful vision of Johnson "at home" are swept away by the breathless telling over of his powers of conversation, "so rich, so animated, and so forcible."

At only one point in the *Life* does Boswell indulge in an essentially unrelieved catalogue of Johnson's most famous and characteristic motions, gestures, and general idiosyncrasies. It is an elaborate rehearsal of all those "singularities" which, when invoked separately, will subsequently give the true Johnsonian stamp to any dramatized anecdote or conversation. Boswell says:

That the most minute singularities which belonged to him, and made very observable parts of his appearance and manner, may not be omitted, it is requisite to mention, that while talking or even musing as he sat in his chair, he commonly held his head to one side towards his right shoulder, and shook it in a tremulous manner, moving his body backwards and forwards, and rubbing his left knee in the same direction, with the palm of his hand. In the intervals of articulating he made various sounds with his mouth, sometimes as if ruminating, or what is called chewing the cud, sometimes giving a half whistle, sometimes making his tongue play backwards from the roof of his mouth, as if clucking like a hen, and sometimes protruding it against his upper gums in front, as if pronouncing quickly under his breath, *too, too, too:* all this accompanied sometimes with a thoughtful look, but more frequently with a smile. Generally when he had concluded a period, in the course of a dispute, by which time he was a good deal exhausted by violence and vociferation, he used to blow out his breath like a Whale. This I suppose was a relief to his lungs; and seemed in him to be a contemptuous mode of expression, as if he had made the arguments of his opponent fly like chaff before the wind. (I, 485–486)

This is the only catalogue of its kind in the *Life,* and it occurs with approximately four-fifths of the book left to go. In its highly concentrated form, it lends power and vividness to each of the characteristic gestures and mannerisms as they are invoked separately throughout the *Life.* Much later in the Wilkes episode, a single phrase can draw upon the full power of the more concentrated images without involving any potentially negative specificity. When Johnson first enters Dilly's drawing room, his consternation and, I think, a completely adequate image of his whole person are conjured up by the final phrase, " 'Too, too, too' ": "When we entered Mr. Dilly's drawing room, he found himself in the midst of a company he did not know. I kept myself snug and silent, watching how he would conduct himself. I observed him whispering to Mr. Dilly, 'who is that gentleman, Sir?'—'Mr. Arthur Lee.'—JOHNSON. 'Too, too, too,' (under his breath,) . . ." (III, 68). In this way, invoked separately or together, Johnson's distinguishing peculiarities play a large part in the dramatic success and power of each anecdote in which they provide the characterizing and appropriate gesture or action.

The dominant mode of representing these aspects of his appearance and mannerisms is that which we have just been describing (although the minor variations are endless): the vast gifts of mind and spirit set off and made all the more remarkable by the uncouth exterior. The archetypal situation—the viewer surprised, perhaps unsettled by Johnson's appearance only to be the more amazed when he begins to speak—occurs sufficiently in the *Life* to have an effect, I think, beyond simply that in the separate instances of it. Reinforced in a less explicit manner throughout the book, it becomes an important fact about our mode of perceiving and responding to Johnson. As we become habituated to the association of images of the sometimes astonishing realities of Johnson's appearance and behavior (his puffings and blowings, etc.) with his great intellectual powers, a sense of interrelation between the two becomes fixed in our minds. The one becomes repeatedly a symbol of the other, and not by accident. Even in the above example, Boswell imagines for us that Johnson's blowing like a whale is a contemptuous gesture, "as if he had made the arguments of his opponent fly like chaff before the wind." If we, as readers, accept the union or the interrelation between these two concepts—the uncouth exterior and the vast intellect beneath—the judicious invocation of any part of our composite image of Johnson's appearance and mannerisms can (as in the example from the Wilkes episode) draw upon the power of the whole. The phrase, "JOHNSON. (Standing upon the hearth rolling about, with a serious, solemn, and somewhat gloomy air)" can project an entirely convincing physical image of the great figure of Johnson and at the same time can unobtrusively but effectively dramatize inner facts about him—rolling about as he rolls a problem about in his mind. The single word "rolling" stamps the scene as authentically Johnsonian, and the physical oddity is in no way reductive of him. Johnson, before we have gotten very far into the *Life,* would not be Johnson without his characteristic gestures. He is individualized most effectively by precisely those famous mannerisms. And his great powers of mind and body would not be so astonishing or remarkable without visualizing them in that way.

Johnson once observed to Boswell, " 'A man should pass part of his time with *the laughers,* by which means anything ridiculous or particular about him might be presented to his view,

and corrected' " (IV, 183). Boswell replied, "He must have been
a bold laugher who would have ventured to tell Dr. Johnson
of any of his particularities." And this response pretty accurately sums up the attitude that must have guided Boswell's
pen as he dramatized scenes and anecdotes involving Johnson's
particularities in the *Life*. It is a bold reader indeed (and I think
an incorrect one) who can read the *Life of Johnson* and laugh
at Johnson for his particularities. Boswell's treatment of Johnson's uncouth appearance and odd mannerisms makes Ho-
garths and porters of us all. We are repeatedly surprised and
delighted by the power of the intellect and the spirit made
to seem all the more remarkable because of the strange and
often uncouth exterior. We come to link the two ideas together
and to recognize and respect them equally as quintessentially
Johnsonian. And when at times the manners are too forcible,
when they become the signs of severe and painful turmoil, we
do not laugh or stare but, like the porter, concede our respect
to the power and the personal force of the man in spite of them.
We respond thus to such material not only because the objective facts of Johnson's life would necessarily and repeatedly
produce such a reaction in us, but because Boswell as a conscious artist and an interpretive biographer actively develops it
in order to create such a response in us. What in the *Tour* he
developed to evoke our sympathetic laughter or smiles, in the
Life he causes to astonish us and make us admire Johnson all
the more.

As is the case with his treatment of Johnson's appearance
and particularities, Boswell's methods for developing incidents
involving Johnson's explosive temper in the *Life* are very different from what they are in the *Tour to the Hebrides*. In the
Life Boswell's literary objective is greater than simply that of
giving us the spectacle of Johnson living up to the popular ideas
about him; it is to challenge those popular ideas, and in some
cases flatly to contradict them. This is especially true where

Johnson's "roughness" is concerned. While his forcible manner
and irascibility were admired and enjoyed by his contempo-
raries, they were also much criticized. They were thought by
some to represent an habitual rudeness, and Johnson was often
censured, in particular, for his occasionally violent attacks upon
his best friends. In the *Tour* Boswell does not formally confront
the problem of Johnson's serious attacks upon friends or outbursts of anger that are painful in human terms. In the *Life*
he feels he must, and he systematically sets about rectifying
what he considers to be the most serious misconceptions con-
cerning what this aspect of Johnson's behavior really demonstrated about his character.

Not all the heated outbursts by Johnson are problematical
or potentially negative. Boswell, perhaps over-sensitive on this
point, repeatedly enjoins us not to wonder at (or censure) Johnson's sallies of impatience and passion when they are provoked
by obtrusive ignorance or presuming petulance; but I think it
is safe to assume that hardly anyone ever has. As we have seen,
Boswell is very good at the light touches needed to make the
obtrusive ignorance or presuming petulance obvious. Thus,
when a pertinacious gentleman "who had talked in a very puz-
zling manner" happens to say to Johnson, "I don't understand
you, Sir,' " and Johnson—his patience at an end—replies, " 'Sir,
I have found you an argument; but I am not obliged to find
you an understanding' " (IV, 313), he is in little danger of being
diminished in our eyes. Quite the contrary. The wit of the retort
alone is enough in most cases to cancel any judgment upon its
severity. But when Boswell records an attack made upon a man
we respect as a friend of Johnson's, and when it is clear that the
attack is made in earnest, it is potentially much more painful,
potentially much more damaging to our estimate of Johnson's
character, and it requires much greater attention and dexterity
on Boswell's part to represent it within the bounds of factuality
and yet in a way that does not diminish and even in some cases
enlarges our admiration for Johnson.

We remember that on several occasions in the *Tour* Boswell reports and comments upon instances of anger or peevishness on Johnson's part in a way that does no real credit to him. The censoring of Johnson's violent remarks about Hume, the report of his fight with Boswell's father, and the other glimpses of simple bad temper are often mentioned only because they occurred or are developed only for the sake of the vividness of the explosion. There is no discernible policy for handling this kind of material artistically in such a way as to neutralize the potentially negative impression it might give about Johnson, or to discuss it in a context greater than that of the fact of its occurrence.

Boswell handles such material very differently in the *Life of Johnson*. He does not housebreak Johnson. Indeed he shows us his forcible spirit and defensive pride in its full fury and of a strength in proportion to the force and violence of all his other thoughts and actions. But instead of showing (as in the *Tour*) simply that explosions sometimes occurred, he concentrates in the *Life* on showing *why*, what they really show us about Johnson and what they do not. As with all his other material in the *Life,* he develops incidents involving Johnson's sometimes violent temper in the context of greater and more impressive facts about his personality and character. Preserving all the vividness of Johnson's tumultuous spirit and its forcible expression in conversation and attack, he represents Johnson's outbursts and anger—even the most serious instances—in ways that always explain them to Johnson's credit and in some cases make them the occasion for powerful images of his greatness of heart.

There are two major ideas about Johnson and his temper that Boswell sets out specifically to combat in the *Life.* The first is that he is naturally and habitually rude (Mrs. Thrale's "natural roughness of manner"). The other and more serious view is that he was indiscriminate in his violence and would readily attack even his best friends with all the venom with which he might have attacked an "American." The first view of Johnson's roughness Boswell most commonly negates by showing (as in the anecdote in which he corrected Mrs. Thrale above) that if Johnson is sometimes impatient it is always and only when he has been provoked by ignorance pretending to knowledge, vanity, etc. This is the way in which he dramatizes all the incidents of this kind in the *Life*. The following example is typical. Boswell reports, "A foppish physician once reminded Johnson of his having been in company with him on a former occasion. 'I do not remember it, Sir.' The physician still insisted; adding that he that day wore so fine a coat that it must have attracted his notice. 'Sir,' (said Johnson) 'had you been dipt in Pactolus, I should not have noticed you'" (IV, 319–320). Boswell makes it clear that the physician was "foppish," that he was foolish and vain of his coat. When Johnson silences him it is not only justified but welcome.

Boswell uses two methods for countering the view of Johnson as sometimes cruel and brutal even to his friends. One is to explain again and again the understandability of Johnson's occasional attacks in light of the great physical and psychological burdens he fought against so heroically all his life. The outbursts are made symptoms of that struggle and not evidence of an essential malice or ill will.[5] The final and most compelling statement of this idea of the "understandability" of Johnson's outbursts is made appropriately in the concluding sketch. Boswell explains: "He was afflicted with a bodily disease, which made

---

[5] Perhaps one of the most vivid explanations of this idea about the understandability of Johnson's outbursts is the one following his seemingly unaccountable snub of Lord Marchmont: "I give this account fairly," says Boswell, "as a specimen of that unhappy temper with which this great and good man had occasionally to struggle, from something morbid in his constitution. Let the most censorious of my readers suppose himself to have a violent fit of the tooth-ach, or to have received a severe stroke on the shin-bone, and when in such a state to be asked a question; and if he has any candour, he will not be surprised at the answers which Johnson sometimes gave in moments of irritation" (III, 345).

him often restless and fretful; and with a constitutional melancholy, the clouds of which darkened the brightness of his fancy, and gave a gloomy cast to his whole course of thinking: we, therefore, ought not to wonder at his sallies of impatience and passion at any time; especially when provoked by obtrusive ignorance, or presuming petulance; and allowance must be made for his uttering hasty and satirical sallies, even against his best friends" (IV, 427).

But the artist in Boswell must have realized that theoretical explanations of what might have been considered a serious flaw in Johnson's character were doubled-edged at best. It was apologizing for Johnson. His most effective way of dealing with such incidents is to dramatize or report them in such a way as to show that the common (stereotypic) view of this aspect of Johnson's behavior does not do justice to him—does not tell the whole story. He confronts the best known instances of Johnson's attacks on his friends directly, to show that when viewed in the proper context, when the whole story is known, Johnson's essential goodness, his fundamental kindness and honesty with himself, make these outbursts merely foils for the greatness of heart and the breadth of compassion that lie beneath these outward manifestations of his brooding and troubled spirit.

He uses the same general formula for developing such material that he had used in developing anecdotes involving Johnson's appearance and particularities: the seemingly forbidding exterior that conceals (from the superficial observer) something much more valuable beneath. As Johnson's uncouth appearance and gestures are forgotten the moment he begins to speak, so his occasional roughness—the result of a troubled mind and spirit—must be forgotten when we see the remarkable degree of humanity and charity that it sometimes masked. As was the case with Johnson's appearance and mannerisms, we are shown Johnson's roughness in all its vividness. Indeed, we are sometimes shown in detail the kind of incidents that are the basis of the false ideas about his rudeness—only to be shown finally how fallacious such a view of his essential nature really is. And, as was the case with the contrast between Johnson's appearance and the vast powers of his mind, his humanity and charity are made to seem all the more remarkable when they are viewed in contrast to the burdens of his proud spirit.

From Boswell's first meeting with Johnson it is clear that Johnson can and does explode, and that the going can be pretty rough. It has often been observed that his first rebuff of Boswell might have crushed many another man and at several points in the *Life* Boswell is to feel not the momentary roughness of Johnson "talking for victory" but an attack in deadly earnest and all the more serious because of its obvious sincerity. One such attack occurs at the first of those times when Boswell presses Johnson too closely about his fear of death. Johnson loses all patience and, genuinely agitated, commands him to stay away. Boswell's development of this scene is typical and particularly helpful in showing what his goals were in actively attempting to control our response to such material. In this instance he first dramatizes the incident itself: "I attempted to continue the conversation. He was so provoked, that he said, 'Give us no more of this;' and was thrown into such a state of agitation, that he expressed himself in a way that alarmed and distressed me; shewed an impatience that I should leave him, and when I was going away, called to me sternly, 'Don't let us meet to-morrow'" (II, 107).

This is a painful moment and a strong and serious rebuff— Boswell makes it quite clear that it is. It is just the kind of incident that makes those who do not know Johnson better accuse him of harshness, even violence to his friends as well as his enemies, and Boswell himself raises the spectre of these misconceptions. But he raises them only to show us how wrong they really are. "I went home," he tells us, "exceedingly uneasy. All the harsh observations which I had ever heard made upon his

character, crowded into my mind; and I seemed to myself like
the man who had put his head into the lion's mouth a great
many times with perfect safety, but at last had it bit off" (II,
107). But we soon discover that if Johnson has the lion's claws
he has his greatness of heart as well. Boswell braves him in his
den the following day, in defiance of the injunction not to meet
tomorrow. Happily he is protected at first by the company of
several others. He is unsure about what mood Johnson will be
in, but the conversation proceeds with no sign of a continuance
of the previous night's hostilities. Finally he dares to approach
Johnson. "I whispered him, 'Well, Sir, you are now in good
humour.' JOHNSON. 'Yes, Sir.' I was going to leave him, and got
as far as the staircase. He stopped me, and smiling, said, 'Get
you gone *in* . . .' " (II, 109).

Boswell knew how this episode ended at the time he wrote it
up for the *Life*. But he presents it in the original sequence and
that is the way we experience it dramatically. We feel the lion's
claws; we wonder perhaps along with Boswell whether the
worst reports about Johnson might not be true, and we are all
the more pleased when they are demonstrated to have been
false. Johnson is indeed a lion—his passions are a lion's passions.
But he is not mean or small. His temper, his fears and defensive
pride were burdens that he labored under all his life, and they
often contributed to his mighty rages. But the point Boswell
makes here is the one he will make again and again—that Johnson's occasional severity did not indicate an *essential* severity, a
bad heart.

Boswell's methods for making this point about Johnson are
not always the same, and in fact one of the most impressive
aspects of his development of this kind of material in the *Life* is
his resourcefulness in dealing with different kinds of artistic
problems. For example, he does not always choose to dramatize
outbursts by Johnson. Sometimes he must have felt that it would
have compromised Johnson in spite of all his efforts to the con-

trary. In such instances, he chooses to weight the scene dramatically in Johnson's favor by dramatizing only the reconciliation. In one very painful scene, also between himself and Johnson, we are *told* that Johnson seemed to have been needlessly cruel to him; but we are *shown* Johnson's reconciliation and apology in detail.⁸

An interesting example of the lengths to which Boswell goes to "set the record straight" about this aspect of Johnson's personality is the following record of a quarrel between him and his long time friend Strahan. It had been an entirely epistolary dispute and therefore did not present the same kinds of problems in terms of dramatizing it that a scene that Boswell witnessed himself would have. Yet he handles it very cleverly in order to make it an occasion for a display not of Johnson's acrimony but of his kindness. He says:

In the course of this year [1778] there was a difference between him and his friend Mr. Strahan; the particulars of which it is unnecessary to relate. Their reconciliation was communicated to me in a letter from Mr. Strahan, in the following words:
"The notes I shewed you that passed between him and me were dated in March last. The matter lay dormant till July 27, when he wrote to me as follows:

'TO WILLIAM STRAHAN, ESQ.
'Sir,
    'It would be very foolish for us to continue strangers any longer. You can never by persistency make wrong right. If I resented too acrimoniously, I resented only to yourself. Nobody ever saw or heard what I wrote. You saw that my anger was over, for in a day or two I came to your house. I have given you longer time; and I hope you have made so good use of it, as to be no longer on evil terms with, Sir,

'Your, &c.
'SAM JOHNSON.'

"On this I called upon him; and he has since dined with me." (III, 364)

_____
⁸ *Life*, III, 338.

Boswell's selective editorial treatment of this material is directly analogous to his practice of selective dramatization. We know from Strahan's letter that he showed Boswell the notes that involved the "particulars" of the argument. But Boswell chooses not to include them, deciding that they are "unnecessary to relate." This is well within the broad limits of truth to fact, since he does record that the quarrel occurred. But in choosing not to go into detail about it he gives special emphasis to the letter of reconciliation which is much more to Johnson's credit. Although he mentions the dates of the respective exchanges, his compression of the incident minimizes any sense of the time lapse between Johnson's attack (in March) and his apology (late in July). The way Boswell handles it Johnson's response seems much more immediate. All our attention is focused on that, and Johnson comes off well there. And while the letter is still fresh in our minds, Boswell rounds off the episode with another anecdote about Johnson's active friendship for Strahan, presumably from another time period in his life: "After this time, the same friendship as formerly continued between Dr. Johnson and Mr. Strahan. My friend mentioned to me a little circumstance of his attention, which, though we may smile at it, must be allowed to have its foundation in a nice and true knowledge of human life. 'When I write to Scotland,' (said he,) 'I employ Strahan to frank my letters, that he may have the consequence of appearing a Parliament-man among his countrymen' " (III, 364–365). This is a neat and effective capstone to the episode. The fact of the genuine warmth of the friendship renewed is emphasized. Not only Johnson's essential goodness and thoughtfulness are shown by the final anecdote, but his "nice and true knowledge of human life" is exemplified as well. In fact, the episode that began as a controlled account of a quarrel with a long-time friend (one that lasted for several months) ends in an image of Johnson's kindness and wisdom.

That Boswell does at times show us Johnson in all his wrath

as well as in all his kindness is one of the most important decisions he made in dramatizing such material in the *Life*. As he observes in another context, "Everything about his character and manners was forcible and violent." His passions, whatever form their expression took, were in direct proportion to the strength and ferocity of all his other physical and mental powers. It is to Boswell's credit that, in deciding to set about contradicting what he considers uncharitable interpretations of Johnson's aggressiveness and roughness he never attempts to "housebreak" him. What an attempt to do so might have resulted in is, I think, anticipated by an observation of the Earl of Eglintoune early in the *Life*. Boswell says:

The late Alexander, Earl of Eglintoune, who loved wit more than wine, and men of genius more than sycophants, had a great admiration of Johnson; but from the remarkable elegance of his own manners, was, perhaps, too delicately sensible of the roughness which sometimes appeared in Johnson's behaviour. One evening about this time, when his Lordship did me the honour to sup at my lodgings with Dr. Robertson and several other men of literary distinction, he regretted that Johnson had not been educated with more refinement, and lived in more polished society. "No, no, my Lord," (said Signor Baretti,) "do with him what you would, he would always have been a bear." "True," (answered the Earl, with a smile,) "but he would have been a *dancing* bear." (II, 66)

Careful throughout the *Life* never to let a suggestion of Johnson's roughness go unchallenged, Boswell observes quickly: "To obviate all the reflections which have gone round the world to Johnson's prejudice, by applying to him the epithet of a *bear,* let me impress upon my readers a just and happy saying of my friend Goldsmith, who knew him well: 'Johnson, to be sure, has a roughness in his manner; but no man alive has a more tender heart. *He has nothing of the bear but his skin.'*" (II, 66).

But tender heart or not, everything about Johnson's character and manners was forcible and violent; and Eglintoune's observation should give us pause for thought. For Boswell to have attempted to housebreak Johnson by playing down or omitting his moments of wrath would have been to attempt to make him a *"dancing* bear." By controlled dramatizations of Johnson "in his wrath"—in all its vividness—but in a way that is not reductive of him and that does not in any way compromise our sense of his greatness, Boswell turns such material into the stuff of one of the most powerful and pleasing literary effects produced by the portrait of Johnson in the *Life*. Professor Bertrand Bronson observes that, "the pervasive sense of what Johnson is keeping in leash, of energy not allowed to run wild, but controlled only by determined and unremitting effort," is what "makes the man so fascinating."[7] We get some of our strongest senses of the extent of that energy and those passions that are being kept barely in check precisely at those moments when they temporarily burst forth. The minor eruption is the index to the power of the volcano. The surprise and sometimes pain in response to the severity of such an outburst only accentuates our sense of the power of the forces within him that Johnson had to struggle with all his life. This is the context in which Boswell puts such incidents in the *Life:* "JOHNSON. . . . (puffing hard with passions struggling for a vent)." Rather than objects for censure (as sometimes in the *Tour*) Johnson's combustibility and aggressiveness are shown in the *Life* to be, in part at least, an inevitable result of the volcanic forces at work within his troubled spirit. He holds them in check as long as he can, and when they explode he does everything in his power to make amends for any injury he has done. They are one more extension of his astounding personal force and emotional power. And when the outbursts are not directed at his friends, when the force and energy within him are released in defense of his most cherished beliefs or in the expression of his deepest fears, they provide some of the most emotionally powerful moments in the *Life:* "DR. ADAMS.

---

[7] Bronson, "The Double Tradition of Dr. Johnson," *Johnson Agonistes and Other Essays*, p. 170.

'What do you mean by damned?' JOHNSON. (passionately and loudly) 'Sent to Hell, Sir, and punished everlastingly'" (IV, 299).

In limiting the discussion here to these specific types of material about Johnson and to the most typical examples of Boswell's development of them two injustices have inevitably been done. A sense of the endless variations in the *Life* upon these basic formulas had to be sacrificed. A very great part of the literary power of the *Life* is the cumulative effect of what Professor Rader describes as the "pleasure of encountering in new and striking but always probable manifestations the astonishing character of Samuel Johnson."[8] Within the larger context of the image of the strengths of Johnson's character to which the various parts of the work contribute, each episode and anecdote is a surprising and different manifestation of those greater truths about him, and only a very imperfect sense of the full power of this aspect of the *Life* could be given here.

Second, in singling out these particular aspects of Boswell's development of materials about Johnson in the *Life* I have obviously had to neglect his treatment of many others which he handled with equal care, and with the same kinds of differences between his development of them in the *Life* as compared with the *Tour*. His development in the *Life* of materials involving Johnson's appearance, particularities, and his violent temper were chosen because the contrast between his treatment in the *Life* and the *Tour* is extremely clear and is, I think, a valid basis for the generalizations I shall make in conclusion about the significance of this aspect of the differences between the two works. Perhaps the most important conclusion to be drawn from the difference between Boswell's treatment of his material about Johnson in the *Life* as compared with the *Tour* is that his great achievement in the *Life* was clearly a conscious one, and clearly

---

[8] Rader, p. 18.

an interpretive act. It was not at all simply the result of the dramatization of a greater amount of material about Johnson in the manner of the *Tour to the Hebrides.*

Johnson's personal heroism in his life-long struggle with the physical and psychological odds against him has always been a major source of the great attraction of the man, and I am not claiming to have rediscovered this important fact. What I am suggesting is that Boswell has not been given sufficient credit for his role as a conscious artist and interpretive biographer in working to produce that kind of response in us. He could not by any stretch of the imagination have invented Johnson's greatness. But in terms especially of the materials we have been discussing here, his treatment of them in the *Tour* shows that he was not compelled to make Johnson's personal greatness as highlighted by these things a major subject of the *Life.*

The artistic choices Boswell makes are very much involved in the creation of the special power of the image of Johnson in the *Life.* A sense of the extent to which this is true can be gotten from some of the responses of the greatest admirers of that Johnson. Let us listen, for example, to the terms of one of Carlyle's strongest responses to that image:

Nature had given him a high, keen visioned, almost poetic soul; yet withal imprisoned it in an inert, unsightly body; he that could never rest had not limbs that would move with him, but only roll and waddle: the inward eye, all penetrating, all embracing, must look through bodily windows that were dim, half-blinded; he so loved men, and "never once *saw* the human face divine!" Not less did he prize the love of men; he was eminently social; the approbation of his fellows was dear to him, "valuable," as he owned, "if from the meanest of human beings:" yet the first impression he produced on every human being was to be one of aversion, almost of disgust. By nature it was farther ordered that imperious Johnson should be born poor: the ruler soul, strong in native royalty, generous, uncontrollable like the lion of the woods, was to be housed, then, in such a dwelling place: of Disfigurement, Disease, and lastly of Poverty which itself made him the servant of servants. Thus was the born king likewise a born slave.[9]

It is exactly the power of the tension between what Carlyle describes in terms of a poetic soul "imprisoned in an unsightly body" that Boswell works actively to create. It is precisely, to use Carlyle's phrase, the image of the "ruler soul," sometimes "uncontrollable" (as in his moments of wrath) but always "generous," that Boswell works to insure that we view in that way. The vividness with which we are made to feel and understand the heroism of this struggle is in direct proportion to the specificity with which Boswell represents the burdens themselves. "What mortal," asks Carlyle, "could have more to war with? Yet, as we say, he yielded not, faltered not; he fought, and even, such was his blessedness, prevailed. Whoso will understand what it is to have a man's heart may find that since the time of John Milton, no braver heart had beat in any English bosom than Samuel Johnson now bore."[10]

If Carlyle (like many another critic and admirer of Johnson) felt the full emotional power of the images of the soul of a poet imprisoned in a grotesque and diseased body—a soul made to seem all the most astonishing because of the contrast with the deformities that impaired it—it is certainly in part because Boswell consistently develops his materials in the *Life* with the intention of creating that kind of image and response. Johnson was sometimes awkward, unkempt, or even ludicrous, but Boswell makes us imaginatively see how "all these particularities were forgotten the moment he began to talk." If, as Carlyle suggests, Johnson's "ruler spirit" was sometimes uncontrollable it was only a sign of the volcanic forces working within; he was generous in proportion.

Carlyle's (and other readers') responses to this important as-

---

[9] Thomas Carlyle, *Critical and Miscellaneous Essays,* Vol. 9 of *The Works of Thomas Carlyle* (London, 1869), pp. 57–58.

[10] Carlyle, p. 93.

pect of Johnson's character in the portrait of him in the *Life* are
as much if not more a response to Boswell's active agency as to
the objective facts of Johnson's life. We could deduce many of
these things from Johnson's own writings and from other biographers' works. But Boswell makes us feel them in dramatic
terms that are much more powerful than the best we could have
done by the power of intellection alone. He creates, to use Professor Rader's words, "an objective correlative of a grand emotive
idea."[11] And what is most significant for our purposes here is that
it is a different objective correlative from the one he created in
the *Tour to the Hebrides*. That is, Boswell's achievement in the
Life is an *achievement* in the truest sense of the word. The *Life*
is a greater work than the *Tour* not because Boswell had more
material about Johnson to work with—more mosaic pieces—but
because he develops his primary factual material differently in
the *Life* than he did in the *Tour*. He does not create Samuel
Johnson in the sense of bringing him into being in his own
imagination. But in seizing upon what is greatest in Johnson's
character and making it the subject of his biography of him (in
defiance of his earlier "version" of him in the *Tour*) he comes
as close to imaginative creation as an artist whose materials are
factual ever can. He takes what were inert factual scraps, as
eligible as any other for deposit in the dustbin of history or col-
lections of "ana," and transforms them into a powerful and universally intelligible image of intellectual brilliance and personal
courage, astonishing in its convincing reality and compelling in
its universality: "Such was SAMUEL JOHNSON, a man whose
talents, acquirements, and virtues, were so extraordinary, that
the more his character is considered, the more he will be re-
garded by the present age, and by posterity, with admiration
and reverence."

---

[11] Rader, p. 8.

CONCLUSION

BOSWELL HAD DIFFERENT literary objectives in each of his major biographical works, and in each his methods for dramatizing his primary factual materials differed accordingly. The works do not represent simply a linear development of the same kinds of literary and dramatic techniques culminating in their perfection in the *Life of Johnson*. They are separate and formally distinct literary achievements, part of whose importance is the versatility they show Boswell to have had in dealing with similar kinds of primary factual material.

The difference between the portraits, especially the two portraits of Johnson, helps more specifically to define the nature of Boswell's very special achievement in the *Life*. And it sheds new light on some of the broader questions about the limits of Boswell's abilities as an artist and biographer. Professor Rader has effectively countered the old notion that Boswell's art in the *Life* was limited by a slavish adherence to chronological arrangement of his data.[1] Perhaps the most important contribution of this comparative study to these broader questions about Boswell's art is the new light it throws upon the old ideas about his art being limited as well because of his zeal for factual accuracy.

Factual accuracy—remarkable factual accuracy—is one of Boswell's great achievements in the *Life of Johnson*. But it was not nearly the limitation upon his interpretive abilities that some[2] have suggested. Professor Waingrow's research reveals that a

[1] Rader, pp. 1–20.

[2] Perhaps as full a statement of this view as any is in Stauffer: "Boswell's passion for truth is not only intense but limited in conception. Truth to him is external and particular. Living as he does so much on the surface of things, believing as he does that the little facts and actions are enough in themselves, the possible relativity of truth could hardly disturb him. His is not the mind of Donne or of Browning or of Shakespeare. His standard is exacting, for he insists upon an almost mechanical perfection" (p. 420).

majority of the materials from which Boswell constructed the
Life were nonverifiable; that his personal journal records account for less than half the materials that went into the making
of it.[3] The most important facts in the *Life of Johnson* were not
empirical facts. Boswell was as concerned if not more concerned
with *interpreting* Johnson's actions as he was with quoting him
correctly or fixing the proper date. Previous critics have given
all the emphasis to his Herculean efforts in the area of verifica-
tion and very little attention to his efforts at interpretation, but
the ideas of factual accuracy and interpretive biography are by
no means mutually exclusive.

Professor Stauffer cites the following as an example of the
kind of fanatical zeal for accuracy that ultimately limited Boswell's art. The anecdote concerns Johnson's helping a gentlewoman across the street and Stauffer shows that Boswell, in the
interest of complete accuracy, makes sure that we understand
that the gentlewoman was "somewhat in liquor" and that the
coin that Johnson gave her was a shilling. On another occasion
Stauffer notes that Boswell shows his master how accurate he
could be by recording details when, writing to Johnson, he relates, "For the honour of Count Manucci, as well as to observe
that exactness of truth which you have taught me, I must correct
what I said in a former letter. He did not fall from his horse . . .
his horse fell with him."[4] That the woman whom Johnson as-
sisted was somewhat in liquor or that Count Manucci fell with
his horse and not from him are certainly bonafide facts. But if
that were the only kind of facts Boswell dealt with in the *Life*
we might assess its value in the way that Johnson did Swift's
Conduct of the Allies when it was observed of it that it had
"strong facts." We might then paraphrase Johnson's retort thus:
" 'Why yes, Sir; but what is that to the merit of the composition? In the Sessions-paper of the Old Bailey there are strong

---

[3] Waingrow, pp. xxii–xxiii.
[4] Stauffer, p. 417.

facts. Housebreaking is a strong fact; robbery is a strong fact; and murder is a *mighty* strong fact: but is great praise due to the historian of those strong facts? No, Sir. [Boswell] has told what he had to tell distinctly enough, but that is all. He had to count ten, and he counted it right' " (II, 65). On the level of direct apprehension I think no one has felt this way about Boswell's achievement in the portrait of Johnson. But when it has come to a more specific explanation of the reasons for the great power of the book, and Boswell's fanaticism about truth and factuality have been looked to for a partial answer, the result has been little more than the idea that one of his greatest virtues was that he counted to ten correctly again and again with a particular flair for dramatizing some of his "facts."

We have seen, however, especially clearly in Boswells' correction of Mrs. Thrale's errors, that facts meant more to him than empirically verifiable data. They meant truths about Johnson's character, and empirical facts tell us little if anything—no matter whether Boswell had to run all over London to fix the date. It is Johnson's actions and what they show us about him that are the important facts, and they must have been subject to any biographer's interpretation. Mrs. Thrale tells us that Dr. Johnson was a gross feeder. But Boswell sees in Johnson's voracious appetite something more interesting and important about his character: "Every thing about his character and manners was forcible and violent; there never was any moderation; many a day did he fast, many a year did he refrain from wine; but when he did eat, it was voraciously; when he did drink wine it was copiously. He could practice abstinence, but not temperance" (IV, 72). Dramatic choices in the development of materials about Johnson's actions *mean* interpretation as surely in Boswell's case as they do in any other biographer's, and it is time Boswell is recognized as having been such an interpretative biographer in every legitimate sense of the word. The great achievement of the portrait of Johnson in the *Life* is a conscious literary achievement—

not that simply of a mirror and tape recorder, but that of an interpretive biographer in control of his materials and of the literary effects he intended to create in the development of them. Professor Stauffer observes that, "The many biographies of Johnson demonstrate that biography is an art rather than a science. The same material, the same incidents, the same anecdotes, are handled by many writers, but the resultant portraits are not the same."[5] This observation is as applicable to Boswell himself as it is to other biographers of Johnson when compared with him, for he too got significantly different results from the same materials in his two portraits of Johnson. It is his *version* of Johnson that has pleased so many for so long. And, as Professor Waingrow observes, "... no matter how many facts are brought to light, Samuel Johnson will always be somebody's hypothesis. And none has pleased so many, or is likely to please so long, as Boswell's."[6]

---

[5] Stauffer, p. 411.
[6] Waingrow, p. 1.

WORKS CITED

Boswell, James. *The Life of Johnson,* ed. G. B. Hill, Revised and Enlarged by L. F. Powell. 6 vols. Oxford, 1964.

Bronson, Bertrand H. "Boswell's Boswell," *Johnson Agonistes and Other Essays.* Berkeley, 1965.

———. "The Double Tradition of Dr. Johnson," *Johnson Agonistes and Other Essays.* Berkeley, 1965.

———. "Samuel Johnson and James Boswell," *Facets of the Enlightenment.* Berkeley, 1968.

Carlyle, Thomas. *Critical and Miscellaneous Essays.* Vol. 9 of *The Works of Thomas Carlyle.* London, 1869.

Dunn, Waldo. *English Biography.* New York, 1916.

Fitzgerald, Percy. *The Life of Boswell.* 2 vols. London, 1912.

Garraty, John. *The Nature of Biography.* New York, 1957.

Johnston, J. D. *Biography: The Literature of Personality.* New York, 1927.

Krutch, Joseph Wood. *Samuel Johnson.* New York, 1944.

Lee, Sir Sidney. *The Principles of Biography.* Cambridge, 1911.

Longaker, Mark. *English Biography in the Eighteenth Century.* Philadelphia, 1931.

Mallory, George. *Boswell the Biographer.* London, 1912.

Nicolson, Sir Harold. *The Development of English Biography.* New York, 1928.

Pottle, Frederick A., and Bennet, Charles H., eds. *Boswell's Journal of a Tour to the Hebrides with Samuel Johnson, L. L. D. Now First Published from the Original Manuscript.* New York, 1936.

Pottle, Frederick A. "James Boswell, Journalist," *Age of Johnson, Essays Presented to C. B. Tinker.* New Haven, 1949.

———. *James Boswell: The Earlier Years, 1740–1769.* New York, 1966.

———. "The Life of Boswell," *Yale Review,* 35 (1946), 445–460.

Pottle, Frederick A., et al., ed. *The Yale Edition of the Private Papers of James Boswell.* 8 vols. New York, 1950–1963.

Rader, Ralph. "Literary Form in Factual Narrative: The Example of Boswell's Johnson," *Essays in Eighteenth Century Biography,* ed. Phillip Daghlian. Bloomington, Indiana, 1968.

Stauffer, Donald. *The Art of Biography in Eighteenth Century England.* Princeton, 1941.

Tinker, C. B. *Young Boswell.* Boston, 1922.

Waingrow, Marshall, ed. *The Correspondence and Other Papers Relating to the Making of the Life of Johnson.* Vol. 2 of the *Yale Edition of the Private Papers of James Boswell,* ed. Frederick A. Pottle, et al. New York, 1969.

Wimsatt, W. K. "James Boswell: The Man and the Journal," *Yale Review,* 49 (1959), 80–92.